Eating for Ireland

First published in 2010 by
Liberties Press
Guinness Enterprise Centre | Taylor's Lane | Dublin 8
Tel: +353 (1) 415 1224
www.libertiespress.com | info@libertiespress.com

Distributed in the United States by
Dufour Editions | PO Box 7 | Chester Springs | Pennsylvania | 19425

and in Australia by
James Bennett Pty Limited | InBooks | 3 Narabang Way
Belrose NSW 2085

Trade enquiries to Gill & Macmillan Distribution
Hume Avenue | Park West | Dublin 12
Tel: +353 (1) 500 9534 | Fax: +353 (1) 500 9595
sales@gillmacmillan.ie

ISBN: 978-1-907593-05-5
2 4 6 8 10 9 7 5 3 1
A CIP record for this title is available from the British Library.

Cover design by Sin É Design
Internal design by Liberties Press
Printed in Ireland by Colour Books

Eating for Ireland

Tom Doorley

For Johann, my other hemisphere

Contents

Foreword

I'm old enough to remember many of the fine – and perhaps not-so-fine – foods Tom Doorley talks about in this wonderful book: Irel coffee, Peggy's leg, Neapolitan ice cream and all the rest. Although some of them are long gone, the memories linger on – not to mention the tastes.

I share Tom's love of food, whether it be plain or elaborate, a quick snack or a proper home-cooked meal, a picnic by the sea or a fantastic meal out in a restaurant, with excellent service and good linen. Food is a key part of who we are as a country, particularly in our current troubled times, and it is important that we encourage an appreciation, indeed love, of it in everybody, particularly the younger generation.

I have to say, however, that the intricacies of tastes, culinary techniques and so on, about which some people wax lyrical, leave me somewhat cold. My wife Kathleen has been known to spend lengthy periods of time discussing with Tom the nuances of the ingredients used in a particular dish, the combination of flavours, and so on. For myself, as Tom says in relation to wine, when it comes to food, I know what I like, and that's that. And he evidently loves mushrooms: reading about them, collecting them, cooking them, eating them. Personally, I will have no truck with the things.

Tom is a wonderful writer with a light touch: reading one of his restaurant reviews is always an entertaining, as well as an edifying, experience. This is a lovely, amusing collection of pieces on all aspects of food and drink. I heartily recommend it to everyone with an interest in the subject.

Gay Byrne

Food is an important part of a balanced diet.

Fran Lebowitz

Introduction

Wallowing in nostalgia is one of life's simplest, cheapest and most guiltless pleasures; if I didn't keep a firm check on myself, I'd do it almost all the time. The great thing about memory, when it's filtered through our nostalgic instincts, is how we manage to skip all the nasty and scary bits of the past. We concentrate solely on the positive, even though it may come with, as a side dish, a sense of loss.

Tastes and smells can transport you way back. The smell of hot tar on an autumn day puts me right back in second class at national school. Not because our beaten hands were dipped in hot pitch, I hasten to add. It's because Griffith Avenue was getting a new road surface at the time.

But the smells and tastes of certain foods are the most evocative. Hot toast. Scorched flour on a baking tray. Sugar being melted to make fudge. A warm tea cosy. Pepper mingling with butter and molten egg yolk. The icing on a coffee cake. Roast beef resting while the gravy is made. All of these, in my mind, conjure up images from my childhood that are so vivid that I can almost reach out and touch them.

This book is largely a collection of memories, with a generous glug of celebration. Celebration of the simple things with which many of us grew up. For good measure, I've added a few things which I only discovered in more recent years.

I want to thank Seán O'Keeffe of Liberties Press for thinking that this would be a good idea, and I also want to thank the whole team there for their unflagging support.

Katrine Olsen doggedly helped to unearth the history of red lemonade and other curiosities. Douglas Appleyard put me right on numerous aspects of the Irish biscuit, and my friends on Twitter – dozens of them – were hugely generous in sharing their own memories, often saving me from my own often imperfect recollections. A big thank-you to all.

Over the years, my various editors at the *Sunday Tribune*, the *Irish Times* and, most recently, the *Irish Daily Mail* have encouraged me to write about food beyond the realms of restaurants. Some of my nostalgic meanderings first saw the light of day in those newspapers.

I am very touched that Gay Byrne, one of my heroes, has so kindly supplied an introduction to this collection of thoughts. I hope they ring a few bells and conjure up some pleasant memories. And if you manage to wallow in a bit of nostalgia, especially in these trying times, I'll be a very happy writer indeed.

Tom Doorley

Sunday breakfast

It's Sunday morning and I'm eight years old. It's late spring or early summer, and it's a bright morning. There are two sounds. The clinking of cutlery and crockery downstairs as breakfast is prepared. And the click-clack of well-polished shoes on the pavement outside as the early Mass-goers take a brisk stroll to the church.

Between that combination of sounds, and the smell of bacon and pudding wafting its way up the stairs, and the warm bed, and the sunlight forcing its way through the curtain and making strange patterns on my bedroom wall, it's all very comforting, all very secure. This is essentially what always happens on the Day of Rest before we go and get fed with the Host. Continuity. Safety.

My mother enjoyed Sunday breakfasts. They were extensive affairs. There would be rashers – always back rashers, cut properly thick, not like the Parma-ham-like stuff we get nowadays. And they were cooked to a crispy sweetness with not even a suggestion of white scum. Nor did they shrink.

And there would be plump sausages, pricked all over with a sharp little paring knife, to avoid explosions on the hot surface of the pan. Sausages that would often be split down the centre and hinged open so as to fit snugly into that great treat, a sausage sandwich.

There would also be black pudding, smooth-textured but for the nuggets of pork fat that lubricated the interior; the kind of pudding that, despite its attractively crunchy surface, could be spread on toast almost like pâté. And white pudding likewise.

There would be fried eggs, done on a very hot pan so that the edges were a little crisp and frizzy, but with molten yolks which were bright orange one moment and then obscured with opacity as my mother spooned a little hot fat over them.

Fried bread was another essential. And it was not just bread tossed into hot fat or oil. My mother used to dip each slice in milk. She claimed that this reduced the fattiness. It may have done, I suppose, but not by much.

The bread that got fried in those days was almost invariably white batch loaf. It was later that we got to eat fried brown soda bread – a delicacy much enhanced by both the taste and texture of a runny fried egg. A meal in itself.

Leisurely as it was, Sunday-morning breakfast did have some degree of urgency to it. Not only did it have to be consumed in time to allow for the mile's walk to the church, but in those days you had to fast for at least an hour before receiving Communion. Everyone checked the time at which they placed the last morsel in their mouth.

Occasionally we would go to early Mass on a Sunday; this expedition would be carried out on an empty stomach. This can't be right, but I seem to remember always returning to the smell of cooking bacon – the most welcoming fragrance in the world.

Tea

I usually drink tea from a mug, ideally a large one. The first tea is poured into me within minutes of rising, but some-times an hour or more before breakfast. Tea is what gets me going in the mornings, and it sustains me into the after-noon.

I believe Tony Benn has a pint mug for his tea, but I expect he has to pace his drinking from it very carefully. The trouble with really big mugs is that the tea is too hot for comfort at first, and then cools rapidly. By the time you get to the last few mouthfuls, the stuff has gone tepid. And tepid tea is no use to man or beast.

Big mugs are handy, though, in one respect. They carry a sufficient amount of tea to see you through having a bath. Whereas a normal-sized mug, taken to the bathroom, causes only frustration.

Occasionally, I have my tea from a fine bone-china cup – usually in the Merrion Hotel, a splendid haven for tea in the afternoon. I realise that a certain amount of ceremony enhances the enjoyment of this great beverage. And on the very few occasions when we use the mid-nineteenth-century tea service that has been handed down through Johann's family, there is simply no doubt about it at all.

When that tea service came into contact with its first splash of tea and crumb of cake, the taking of tea in the afternoon involved larruping into bread and butter, possi-bly cucumber or cress sandwiches, a slice of Victoria sponge, a nibble of fruit cake and possibly even scones with jam and cream. This was in the days when the cooked breakfast was compulsory (no other kind was known), luncheon was a three-course meal, and dinner, at about eight o'clock, would involve soup, fish, main course, cheese, pudding and savoury. Unless you were entertaining, in which case you would add a few courses.

Over the years, we have come to eat less, and to exercise less; the tea ceremony has been replaced by the mug in the kitchen with a few ginger nuts for dunking. So much for progress. But every now and then, it's worth reviving the proper tea ceremony in the late afternoon.

Make a few rounds of cucumber sandwiches (the only things in the whole world to justify the existence of modern sliced pan). Peel the cucumber, slice it very thinly and season with just a hint of salt and freshly ground pepper, preferably white. And don't even think of using anything other than good Irish butter. Trim the crusts off.

Make scones, and serve them warm from the oven with thick cream (or clotted cream if you can get it) and home-made jam, preferably raspberry. Of course, people have come to blows over the sticky question of what goes on first: the jam or the cream. My view on this is clear. Just try doing both and you will know that jam *has* to go on first. Otherwise you will end up trying to get the jam to adhere to the cream, which is as fruitless an exercise as King Canute's well-known request to the sea. (And do remember that 'home-made' doesn't have to mean made by you.) We often add a sticky gingerbread cake into the equation.

I tend to favour the smoky flavour of lapsang souchong in the afternoon, but you may find that it comes as a bit of a shock to your guests. This is not a time for tea bags. Tea bags are devices created by Satan himself: because the tea is finely milled, it will stew very quickly and become unbearably tannic. I don't care if the great tea experts disagree. They are trying to sell the things anyway. Tea bags are not as evil as instant coffee, but they are far from benign. And why do the really cheap ones taste of machine oil? I think I'd prefer not to know.

So whatever sort of tea you choose, be sure that you use the leaf version, and that you warm the pot thoroughly before brewing. Never re-boil the water; it must be absolutely fresh. Put in the tea and pour on the freshly boiled water, but don't stir until the tea has had a chance to draw for a few minutes. Then let the leaves settle and pour through a tea strainer (something that was once to be found in every household but is now largely confined to jumble sales and antique shops).

Some people like to put their milk in first. To me, this is the kind of genteelism, like sticking up your little finger as you drink from the cup, that makes me physically wince. It's 'naice' and 'refained'. And it makes me want to scream. But it's up to you.

Actually, it also affects the taste of the tea. I'm not sure why this is – maybe the hot tea briefly raises the temperature of the milk beyond a certain point – but milk-first tea has a slightly sweeter, vaguely caramel-like taste that I simply don't fancy.

Some of the milk-first tendency claim that this bizarre practice is based on respect for fine china. The suggestion is that it's a way of protecting your ancient Spode from the shock of hot tea. I don't know who came up with this daft notion, but I'm morally certain that no china tea cup has ever been shattered by a splash of scalding Darjeeling. No, I'm afraid it's a class issue.

Porridge

Not very long ago, when I was staying in a very pleasant hotel in the west of Ireland, I ordered porridge for breakfast. And when it arrived, I had the opportunity to break with the habit of a lifetime. It was served with a little jug of warm honey on the side.

Sweet porridge? This was not something that was ever eaten in my family, although I married into one where it was the usual thing. I toyed with the idea of ignoring the honey and simply fortifying the porridge with a modest dose of salt, but then I thought again. Try anything once, as they say, except incest and folk dancing.

And so I drizzled on the warm honey. (It has to be warm, otherwise it will be too thick to distribute over the surface of the gloopy cereal.) And I tucked in.

It was fine. It was certainly very different. It was, in a strange way, comforting. Indeed, it reminded me of something from very long ago. I must have had it, or something like it, when I was very small. And for some reason I had a flashback to when I was five years old or less, being led by the hand to the Froebel school in Eccles Street. I suspect I had been set up for the day with . . . sweet porridge!

Memory plays lots of tricks, but I imagine I was converted soon after that to the salty version. The appeal was complex: there was a nuttiness, a chewiness to the pinhead oatmeal that made our porridge more textured than the pap you get if you use rolled oats.

In those days, milk came in glass bottles, and by the time you got to removing the foil cap (provided the local birds had not pecked a hole in it), there was a fine layer of cream at the top. This was what went on the porridge, and when it was poured you got a combination of milk and lovely, slightly yellowish cream, which appeared in swirls.

Having given the bowl a stir, the salt would start to migrate into the creamy milk and the whole thing became a rich, savoury, warming combination. How such simple materials could become a delicious meal was a constant source of wonder. In a sense, this was my first experience of a dish becoming much more than the sum of its parts. A kind of alchemy.

Porridge has the great virtue of feeding you well for very little money. And as carbohydrates go, it releases its energy quite slowly, so the benefits and the sense of – I love this word – *satiety* are pleasantly persistent. I mean, you feel full for quite a while.

Flahavan's was the porridge with which I grew up. I remember when they got into terrible trouble over a radio commercial. We were already familiar with their TV ad, which showed very cold and wet people clambering on to a crowded bus (one of the old ones with the open platform at the back), and their slogan, which started: 'When there's a *brrr* in the month . . . '

But then they had the temerity to suggest that the winters were very cold and damp in Donegal, and that this was why Flahavan's had a big following up there. The people of Donegal were outraged. If Joe Duffy had been running *Liveline* in those days, the subject would have fuelled the programme's sense of indignation for days.

As it was, Flahavan's went back to images of cold, wet

people, but in a less geographically defined area. And everyone was happy again, and headed off to work or school with a tummy full of hot oatmeal.

Toast

When I say that bread was the staff of life in our house when I was little, I don't mean the white sliced pan and Slimcea that, for some reason, took the 1960s by storm. I remember Darina Allen saying that it was always shop bread that was wheeled out when visitors arrived, especially clerical ones.

In our household, we ate a lot of brown soda bread. This was made with sour milk (milk used to go sour in those days, instead of just turning foul and disgusting) and fashioned into a round, flat loaf with four distinct quarters marked by the knife before it went into the oven.

But we also had white bread. White soda bread never really did it for me. It was just a bit too dense. OK, the harm was taken out of it by the judicious application of strawberry jam. That added lubrication made it seem more like a scone than a slice of bread.

Bread was delivered every day by the man from Boland's with the slow-moving electric van, in the back of which were lots and lots of well-worn wooden trays. And the bread of choice, I'm happy to say, was the batch loaf.

If you have never encountered a batch loaf, I'm not at all sure how I can begin to describe it for you. For a start, it's shaped more or less liked a cube, with a dome of well-browned (virtually burnt) crust on top. Its sides always seemed to be adorned with what I can only call flakes of bread, which could be pulled off very readily and popped straight into the mouth.

The bread itself had rather more substance than the

sliced pan which I would occasionally be fed in other, less fortunate people's houses. While very fresh white sliced pan would vanish almost into thin air upon being chewed (and it has not got any better in the meantime), you always knew, with the batch loaf, that you were eating bread.

Batch loaves have a tendency to go, if not quite stale, a little denser after their first bloom of freshness. And it is at this stage, perhaps, that they really come into their own, for this is when they make, arguably, the best toast.

We were a somewhat Luddite household, as were many in the 1960s and 1970s. Gadgets were relatively expensive in those days, and as a result dedicated toasters were something of a rarity. We used to stick bread under the grill or, less often but more excitingly, onto a fork, which would then be held in front of the fire.

My father, who was essentially Victorian (although he was actually born during World War One), greatly liked the notion of toastings things, especially crumpets, in front of the fire. And he acquired, or perhaps inherited, at least two proper toasting forks in the course of his life.

One of them, in lovely old brass, is telescopic. This is used mainly to toast marshmallows these days, but I still remember the excellent toast, always with a faint suggestion of coal-smoke, that came from its sooty prongs.

It's a bit of a skill, toasting in front of a real fire. Get too close, and the bread bursts into flames; stay too far away, and it dries out. It's important to remember, too, that there is quite a distinction between something that is toasted and something that is burnt. Carbon is not much fun. And burnt bread tastes bitter – no matter how hard you try to scrape off the charcoal with the back of a knife.

I suppose it was because my salad days were spent in a slightly frugal era that toast was almost always made with bread that was past its best. It was a way of using up the stuff rather than letting it go mouldy and useless.

So toast varied. If the bread had dried out too much, the toast would shatter as soon as you tried to butter it. The best toast was made from bread just on the cusp of staleness. No, actually, the best toast was made from fresh bread, but we only got that (usually with Bovril) if we were sick.

There is, of course, a special category of toast which, unless you have tasted it yourself, sounds just like the ordinary version. This is Aga toast. Aga toast is made by placing your slice of bread inside a device that looks like a hinged round tennis racket made of wire mesh, and then sticking it under the lid of the hotplate. If the Aga is good and hot, the bread will toast very quickly and develop a texture and character that only this form of cooking seems to be able to achieve.

My favourite bread for the Aga treatment is the turnover. This is not entirely unlike the batch, but the crust is more delicate and its shape, in profile, looks a bit like the letter 'L'.

The heat of the hotplate makes a slice of fresh turnover seem both crunchy and fluffy at the same time. And if that isn't the ultimate form of toast, I don't know what is.

The decline of the Irish sausage

There's nothing like nostalgia for helping you to get it wrong. When I look back fondly on far-distant breakfasts, I may be mistaken in thinking that the sausages were always plump, glistening, meaty and perfectly seasoned with the magical mixtures known only to the best butchers. But I'm pretty sure I'm right.

I will never forget my first encounter with an inferior sausage. It looked all wrong from the start. It was too . . . I'm not sure . . . perfect and angular. And it had a kind of dull surface, with no glistening to mention.

Inside, although fully cooked, it was pink. And the texture . . . dear me, the texture was like a cross between cake and melted fat. Which is probably pretty much what it was, in effect.

In the good old days, sausages were meaty things which needed to be pricked before they went into the pan. Otherwise the melting fat (and yes, there was a lot of fat) and the rising internal temperature would cause an explosion, in which underdone minced pork would be scattered over all four walls of the kitchen. And yes, sausages were fried. I can't remember when my family took to grilling them, but I suspect it might have been at the dawn of the health-conscious 1980s. Breakfast, when I was a child, involved a pan. Always. And sometimes two of them.

The American writer Michael Pollan advises us to avoid eating anything that would be unknown to our grandparents. Well, put like that, this is a recipe for a pretty dull existence. My grandparents knew nothing about polenta, and I'm not sure they were at all up to speed on the benefits of garlic. I think Mr Pollan means that we should keep our diets free of stuff that had not been invented by the time our grandparents came along. Put like that, it's sound advice.

So don't eat sausages. Granny wouldn't recognise them.

There are probably several reasons for the decline of the sausage. One is the general drive towards making as much food out of as little raw material as possible. Hence the way sausages are packed with filler rather than pork. The other has to do with the horror which we have developed, with the aid of certain vast commercial interests, of fat. Instead of acknowledging that sausages are as much about fat, if not more so, than about meat, and that they are therefore not an ideal part of the daily diet, people still madly want to have their sausage, but with reduced fat. Not possible. Something has to give.

Of course, there are people making proper sausages, and it's remarkable how a butcher's skill can turn the dull, lacklustre meat that passes for commercial Irish pork into something really worth putting under the grill. But such sausages are not easy to find. Research and local intelligence are needed.

I don't know what it would take to make your average, industrial modern sausage (which seems to have more rusk in it than meat) explode. But blowing it up would be a whole lot more fun than eating it.

Coffee

I quite like coffee experts. There is so much to be known about the subject, and yet they wear their knowledge lightly. I often wonder why we have wine columnists and, as far as I can gather, no coffee columnists. Maybe the coffee experts realise that most normal human beings find the minutiae of such subjects unbearably tedious.

I can get quite excited – no, perhaps I should say 'moderately interested' – in *terroir* and vine clones and drip irrigation, but having written about such things for longer than any other wine commentator in the country, I've decided that only the terminally anorakish could possibly find such things interesting. I now take the same view towards coffee. I'm pretty sure there are two varieties of coffee plants (Robusta and Arabica), and that how much roasting you give the beans is important. Beyond that? I'm sorry, but I don't think my life will be greatly enhanced by knowing the rest.

I'm like one of those people who drive wine writers mad by saying, often with a slightly inane grin: 'I don't know much about wine, but I know what I like!' Well, I know what I like when it comes to coffee. I like espresso to be intense and bitter; not too hot, but much more than just warm. I like a cappuccino that is in no danger whatsoever of being confused with a *café au lait*, and if I'm drinking a mug of black, unsweetened coffee, I like it dark, rich and reasonably rounded. The stuff that the coffee experts describe as 'fruity' I find either to be the equivalent of Beaujolais or just deadly dull.

So yes, I'm a bit of a coffee savage. I'm like the eejit who drinks only Australian Shiraz and who would more than likely spit out a Burgundy if he were to take a mouthful by accident. But I like my coffee made really well, using water at the correct temperature and a squeaky-clean machine. This rarely happens in Ireland. Indeed, my favourite coffee establishment (which had better remain nameless) serves complete rubbish. I go there for the chat and the likelihood of bumping into friends. The normal stuff is bad enough, but on the one occasion I ordered a decaf I thought I might be sick. Right there, on the spot.

When I was growing up, all of us Dubliners knew about coffee beans because Bewley's in Grafton Street had, in their shop window, a machine for roasting them. And when Bewley's stopped roasting on the premises, one of the great aromas of Dublin vanished into thin air. The nearest you will get to it these days is the haunting perfume that wafts down from St James's Gate when they're roasting the barley at what my grandfather always referred to as 'the Brewery'.

Now, while I knew about coffee beans from my earliest days, I didn't encounter one close up until many years later. Coffee came in two forms. There was the instant stuff – Maxwell House, in our case – and Irel, a thick, sweet coffee syrup (I think it may, at one stage, have contained chicory), to which you could add boiling water and have . . . well, a type of drink.

We didn't drink Irel or Camp, the British equivalent, in our household. They were used to make the icing for coffee-and-walnut cake, the mainstay of Sunday-afternoon tea if visitors were expected.

At first, instant coffee came in the form of a fine powder. Then it was decided to process the powder into 'granules', presumably because it would look somewhat less unattractive in this form. Some misguided soul may even have thought that it would look more like real coffee.

The advent of coffee granules did nothing for the taste of instant coffee. It was, and always has been, beyond redemption. But there were some forms of the stuff that tasted less unpleasant: Blend 37 and Gold Blend, both from Nescafé. In my early teens, I weaned my parents on to these rather more expensive brands, arguing that, considering how little coffee was drunk in our house, the additional expenditure would hardly be vast.

You need to be my age or older to appreciate that, for a long time, real coffee was regarded as highly exotic and, in practical terms, very difficult and fiddly to make. I remember, back in the 1970s, the late Clement Freud suggesting that you should take one or two coffee beans and put them under the grill so that the magical aroma would waft out to impress the guests at your dinner table – then make a pot of Blend 37. You know, it probably worked: the smell of roasting coffee is so much better than the taste of the stuff. It's the same with Gitanes. They smell great in the open air – very Gallic and evocative – but the senses are not nearly as grateful if you actually go and smoke one.

One innovation of the 1970s brought real coffee a little closer, at least in theory. This was the coffee bag. This was like a tea bag, only filled with very finely ground coffee. The great advantage was that you could make coffee just as easily as you could make tea. The disadvantage was that the coffee always tasted stale and weak. But it was still better than the average instant.

My last memory of coffee bags is this. My mother had made a big pot with the things. As she lifted it to pour, the body of the pot parted company from the base, which remained on the table. Hot coffee and sodden coffee bags went everywhere, and I was left, rather illogically, with a lasting distrust of the things.

By the time I was at university, the plunger pot had arrived. While most students lived on Pot Noodles and Lucozade, there were some, especially as we hit the Sophister years, who took on the mantle of sophistication by doing things like brewing real coffee in their rooms. An Athena poster on the wall and a coffee pot by the stove: that was the Trinity style of the day. Regular pilgrimages to Bewley's would be made – usually for the smallest quantity of coffee that could be dispensed.

And even then, I'm not sure I knew anyone who had a coffee grinder. I realise now that my wife's family down in County Meath had had one for decades, but it was a manual affair and it must have taken days to produce enough to make a potful.

When we got married in 1984, we got the usual combination of useful and useless gifts. But the two great survivors are a couple of cast-iron casseroles, which are in almost daily use, and a Bodum plunger pot, which has been retired to our Dublin flat, where, with its second replacement glass, it still regularly gives sterling service.

Of course, the plunger pot was the Nespresso of its day. As for such machines, we got an Illy espresso maker years ago. It still works, and we have enough gadgets in the house. It makes a fine espresso but, just as is the case in so many cafés, it would make an even better one if we managed to clean it regularly.

Where have all the rashers gone?

Call that a rasher? That mean little waif-like slice of cured pig meat? That rindless scrap which will shrink to a fifth of its not-terribly-impressive original size upon exposure to the grill? That is not a rasher. It's a sliver.

And it's not just any old sliver. It has been so pumped up with water, and the various agents required to keep the water from escaping again, that it will not so much grill or fry but steam. And in doing so will produce white scum. And while white scum is now regarded as perfectly normal in rasher-eating circles, I am old-fashioned enough to think that it has never been part of what you might call the Essentials of Bacon (with apologies to Sir Francis).

The rashers I remember best were far from slivers. They were manly slices, tranches really, cut from a whole side of bacon by the butcher while you (your mum, really) waited. They were closer to being thin bacon chops than the micro-tomed stuff you get in vacuum packs these days.

I don't know if they were wet-cured or dry-cured back then, but I do know that the rashers of the 1960s were never too salty, and they cooked to a meaty crispness. The rinds were thick enough to puff into a fabulous savoury honeycomb of crunch that would put you in mind of pork scratchings.

Even the best of the modern rashers are sliced far too thinly. Maybe it started as a ruse to make us think we were getting more for our money. But by now it has become a

fashion. I'm not sure you could even sell thickly cut rashers these days.

You know, I sometimes think that it's not just concerns
about healthy eating that has demoted the 'full Irish breakfast' to the status of an occasional indulgence. No, it's the
fact that the rashers are swimming in white scum and the
sausages are like extruded styrofoam.

Fancy a croissant and coffee?

Tomato ketchup

One of my favourite dishes – and this dates from way back in infancy – is very crunchy chips (the sort that have been cooked a little too cool and a little too long) with a fried egg or two on top. Very carefully fried. These eggs need to be cooked, of course, but only just. A very runny yolk is a must.

Now, this is a great combination. Simple and delicious, even if it's not likely to win a place in a healthy-eating competition. But there is a little something that can make it even better – that can take it, indeed, into celestial realms. And that's tomato ketchup. Heinz, to be precise.

Actually, when I was growing up, we didn't call it 'tomato ketchup'. In our house, it was always called 'tomato sauce' – which, when you think about it, is a different class of thing entirely. I mean, tomato sauce? That's what goes onto a pizza base. Or is tossed with spaghetti. You wouldn't do either with ketchup, surely? (Actually, in Holland, Venezuela and Japan, ketchup with pasta is quite popular. But I digress.)

Ketchup, as I'll call it in the interests of clarity, was not a big feature in my childhood. It was regarded with a smidgen of suspicion because (a) it was manufactured, presumably in a factory, and (b) it was, or appeared to be, American. But, leaving those considerations on one side, it was tolerated.

And I think the toleration may have been because of me and my lack of appetite. Anything that made me eat, or at least encouraged me to do so, was A Good Thing. And I do remember wielding the ketchup bottle.

I fear it may not have been Heinz, the best of them all. I seem to remember a picture of a French chef from central casting on the label, so I'm assuming that it was, indeed, Chef Tomato Ketchup – which is still around.

For me, it enhanced mashed potatoes, was indispensable with fish fingers (when I could be persuaded to eat them), was highly desirable with egg and chips and, curious as it may seem, was good as an occasional sandwich filling. The latter is a childhood taste experience after which I don't hanker these days. I think my mother confined her use of ketchup to making the pink Marie Rose sauce that went, just as religiously as a dusting of paprika, with prawn cocktail at Christmas time.

Ketchup goes back a long way and evolved, more than likely, as a means of preserving the goodness of fresh tomatoes through the long, dark winter days. So, it all started with home-made ketchup, or 'catsup', long before such stuff was branded.

The first known recipe for ketchup – or however you want to spell it – appears to be the one in *The Compleat Housewife or Accomplished Gentlewoman's Companion*, written by a Mr Smith and published in 1727. It was for 'English Katchop' and involved anchovies, shallots, white wine, white vinegar, horseradish and oodles of spices. But, as you may have noticed, no tomatoes.

Heinz started up more than a century later in Pittsburgh, Pennsylvania. It was, initially, very much an artisan business. The 'factory' was a small shed surrounded by a garden of just under an acre. The workforce, comprising two women, made both walnut and tomato ketchup, the latter being sold loose out of old whiskey barrels for twenty-four cents a gallon. But their 'Extra Fine Catsup' sold for vastly more.

The original Heinz business went bust in the 1870s, but it was revived as H. & J. Heinz. By 1900, it was the biggest ketchup producer in the world, and by the eve of World War One they were selling $2.5 million worth of the stuff annually.

Part of this phenomenal success can be ascribed to Heinz's decision to avoid chemical preservatives. Benzoate of soda was widely used in the early ketchup industry, and Heinz relentlessly advertised the fact that their product was additive-free.

I've never made ketchup myself, because when we have a glut of tomatoes in the garden, the simplest thing is to skin them and seed them, then cook the pulp down to reduce it in size and intensify the flavour. Then it can go into small containers and straight into the freezer.

I have, however, tasted a few home-made versions. While many of them were very pleasant in a vaguely ketchupy way, none of them did quite what Heinz does when I apply it to my egg and chips.

And what *does* it do? Well, it's sharp and slightly sweet, quite salty and savoury, and there's a kind of appetite-enhancing twang to it which is not unlike what you get from the better kind of pickle. It also comes out of a branded jar, so it has to be a vaguely guilty pleasure.

Various ketchups have their fans, but I tried a few of the other big brands when I was planning to write this book, and I have to say I was not impressed. No, it's Heinz for me.

I once saw a waiter filling Heinz bottles with generic ketchup, and I wondered if anyone would be fooled. Cheap ketchups tend to be darker and – I never thought I would use the phrase in this context – very one-dimensional by comparison.

There is one other use for Heinz tomato ketchup, and it is one which I blush to reveal. Many years ago, I was introduced to a very special toasted sandwich by one Robbie O'Neill, who is now a distinguished barrister. It involved a combination of Cheddar cheese, garlic salami and a generous dollop of ketchup.

Sealed inside that crisp sandwich exterior, with its molten heart of scalding ketchup, was a combination of flavours that sang to me. Especially after pints. Some day, I will retrieve the sandwich toaster, which I strongly suspect has gone to boarding school with one or other of my children, and recreate this uncompromising toasted sandwich.

The lunchbox

When I remember what I ate at school, I'm amazed that I survived into adulthood. I can't say, of course, what mental scars remain.

We were fed industrial-grade oxtail soup, bread rolls which were better adapted for use as missiles (and believe me, they were employed as such), and slices from a giant mince pie. It was a most bizarre diet. Little wonder, then, that most of us refuelled at the tuck shop, where crisps, minerals, chocolate and sherbet fountains supplemented the swill from the refectory. At least it was a day school.

These days, the whole notion of 'healthy eating' seems very dreary. I don't mean the regular consumption of healthy foods, and a general balance to the diet. I mean the 'healthy eating' mantra. When some bloody nutritionist starts up about minimising fat and reducing salt, I turn off. The first requirement to qualify as a nutritionist seems to be a complete lack of interest in food. The second is a bullying, bossy manner.

I don't know how I would have reacted to a healthy lunch during my schooldays. Let's just say that the issue never arose. My children are very happy to munch raw carrots, but I suspect I would have been deeply suspicious of anything that didn't come garishly wrapped and with a large dose of refined sugar. Sugar was what I craved above all else during the school day.

These days, of course, there are more kids who have been brought up on proper food, but they still relish the thoughts of junk. How many twelve-year-olds will make the healthy choice when confronted with a packet of crisps, on the one hand, and a bowl of salad on the other? The best you could hope for would be that they might eat both.

Everyone wants their children to eat a healthy diet, but we have to lead by example. This is harder than it may sound. Far too many adults eat what they regard as a healthy diet and get no fun or pleasure from it whatsoever. And being grown-ups, they are used to doing things because they are supposed to be good for us, rather than for sheer joy. Kids are not like that. And you know something? They're absolutely right.

A healthy diet that makes you miserable is a contradiction in terms. It's not healthy at all. Healthy food must be packed with exciting flavours to wow the taste buds.

The ground rules are simple, of course. You want a lot of complex carbohydrate (fruit, vegetables, wholegrain bread), a certain amount of protein (pulses, cheese, lean meat) and a small amount of fat. You don't need refined sugar, and would be much better off without it.

Hummus, the Middle Eastern chickpea puree, is one of the healthiest, most nutritionally complete things you can eat. But it has to be unapologetic about its taste – hence lots of lemon and garlic and sesame-seed paste.

Take a can of chickpeas, two fat cloves of garlic, the juice of a lemon, a large dessertspoonful of tahini (sesame-seed paste, from health-food stores), a little salt and plenty of freshly ground black pepper. Place all of this in the food processor and whizz until you have a puree. You will probably need to add a little water until you get the right consistency. Scoop it up with toasted pitta bread.

Now, here's a strange thought. A salad of celery and apple with maybe a little grated onion and carrrot, tossed very lightly in mayonnaise which has been thinned with lemon juice, becomes a complete meal if you add toasted walnuts or pine nuts (or both, for that matter).

We all need calcium, but kids can't get enough of it. This is where yoghurt comes in, even at lunchtime. Thick Greek yogurt drizzled with honey and sprinkled with muesli (brought in a separate container) may be rather like breakfast, but when did that ever bother children? Stewed blackberries stirred into yoghurt makes good, healthy eating – and a really scary colour.

We shouldn't forget, of course, that children can eat a lot more cheese than sedentary adults. Slivers of really good mature Cheddar or Parmesan go very well with a crunchy, sweet apple.

Extravagance is sometimes called for. A ripe, juicy mango eaten with a sprinkling of lime juice is indescribably good. A whole punnet of autumn raspberries with a little thick yoghurt is almost the definition of luxury. And, speaking of fruit, make sure you buy well ahead, because the likes of bananas and peaches are rarely sold ready to eat.

You can make healthy crisps fairly easily. Just scrub the spuds, slice very thinly, place on a baking tray and brush very lightly with olive oil. Place in the top of a very hot oven for ten minutes (but keep checking them). Let them cool, sprinkle with a little salt and put into an airtight container. They have much more fibre and far less fat and salt than the commercial versions.

My children adore fresh organic carrots and even ask

for them from time to time – not because they are a healthy option but because they have great texture and a wonderful taste. They need to be crisp, crunchy and sweet – not the woody old things that all too often masquerade as the real thing. And they're fun!

That's how kids approach healthy eating. If we did the same, I reckon we would all be healthier and happier. Good, healthy food is always fun. Nutritionists are not.

Tayto

A *package* of crips. It's very odd, but a lot of people say that. At least according to Ray D'Arcy, who probably knows about these kinds of social phenonmena.

I'm not sure how much truth there is in this, but there's a strong suggestion that one of Ireland's greatest culinary contributions to the world was the creation of cheese-and-onion potato crisps in 1954. Tayto dates from then. I'm told that, before this date, crisps were seasoned only with salt, and that the salt was supplied in a little bag within the bag (or 'package', come to think of it).

The strength of the smell and the flavour of Tayto cheese-and-onion crisps is legendary. When I was at national school, a single packet – or package – could scent an entire classroom. And I mean a classroom containing forty boys, each contributing his own ripe aroma to the atmosphere.

In theory, cheese-and-onion crisps are vile. They taste of neither cheese nor onion but of some pungent other combination about which it is possibly best not to think. Salt-and-vinegar crisps, straightforward and innocent in their simplicity, are timid and anamemic by comparison.

But cheese-and-onion crisps, despite their ability to knock out the entire complement of your taste buds, are delicious. They are the most savoury thing you can put in your mouth.

There are all sorts of crisps these days, from the aggressively middle-class variations on sea salt and cracked black pepper to the chemistry-set echoes you get with anything claiming to involve a pickle. There are even Thai-flavoured crisps – which, oddly enough, have not been a great success in Thailand. But one thing is sure. Tayto cheese 'n' onion is the original and the best. And they offer amazing value. You can still taste and smell them days, sometimes weeks, after consuming them.

Extinct sandwiches

I lived through an era when Dualit toasters were not trendy and could be bought only from vendors of catering equipment. I remember when toasted sandwiches contained either plastic cheese or plastic ham, or, if you were really unlucky, both. They were placed in cellophane bags, as if to underline their very remote connection with actual food, and placed under the grill. Meanwhile, your pint was settling.

There was nothing wrong with the Lincoln Inn when I was at Trinity. It did a fine pint, it was a kind of extension of the junior common room in Regent House, and its maître d' (who went on to own the Blue Light in Barnacullia) was a fine host. But it was not noted for its food. The soup was reminiscent of school (and I wonder if that phrase has *ever* been used in a good way), while the toasted sandwiches were constructed and 'cooked', if that's the word, along the lines which I have outlined above.

More elaborate establishments attempted to raise the bar for the toasted sandwich in the cellophane bag. The collective genius of Irish publicans came up with the 'toasted special' – and here I would urge younger readers, if there are any, to bear in mind that the word 'special' had a much broader meaning when I was, allegedly, undergoing third-level education.

The toasted special involved, if you like, the baseline ingredients of plastic cheese (we are talking the essence of Easi-Single here) and the kind of ham that is so shiny you could use a slice as a shaving mirror. To this was added slices of onion. White onion, of course: there was no such thing as red onion in those days. Red onion? I ask you! What will they make up next?

The onions would, of course, be matured so as to extract the maximum amount of sulphurous fumes. In some establishments, this would take place on a chopping board somewhere towards the back of the premises; in more thorough places, maturation was concluded within the actual sandwich itself – a process which imparted a distinctive tang to the finished product. A tang that could, in certain circumstances, bring a tear to the eye – rather like pulling your own nasal hair very hard.

The final ingredient, the *coup de grâce* (or cup of grease), was the addition of sliced, carefully unripened tomatoes, which, once again, had been given time to relax.

Such sangers had a function – the buffering of pints – and they did the trick up to a point. But they did not evoke a love of toasted sandwiches, even in a nostalgic way. (Although I have to say that Morrissey's of Abbeyleix produce a 'toasted special' that is, relatively speaking, of Michelin quality. And I don't mean rubbery.)

I looked askance at the toasted sandwich until I was introduced to a remarkable version by one Robbie O'Neill, then a TCD student and a talented wielder of the electric sandwich toaster. The details appear under the entry for 'Tomato ketchup'.

I think we can be sure that a sandwich made of white sliced pan, generously anointed with soft butter, and with cheese-and-onion crisps, was not invented by a nutritionist. Nor would it find a place amongst those dishes recommended by the late Dr Atkins. But there's no doubt about it, it's a terrific combination. And no matter how long it is since you've had one, I bet you want one now.

Putting on the Ritz

My parents were not keen on things American. Indeed, despite the fact that many of their relations lived in the United States, the word 'American' was often used in a somewhat derogatory way. It seemed to refer, somehow, to all those things about which Archbishop John Charles McQuaid was constantly warning us.

But there were exceptions, of course. *National Geographic* magazine was A Good Thing – and certainly a lot glossier and more colourful than anything produced on this side of the Atlantic. And Ritz crackers. Not that we were particularly aware that they were originally from the United States.

Invented in the early 1930s by a Mr Ritzman, and marketed by the giant Nabisco company, they were, and still are, small, salty, crunchy and curiously tasty. So popular is the original Ritz cracker (the range has, like everything else, been 'diversified') that it even has its own Facebook page. But what hasn't, I suppose?

Anyway, Ritz crackers, with their four grammes of fat in every little one, was a mainstay in our househould. They would be spread with cheese, pâté or even, just to boost the fat content, butter. They are forever associated in my mind with steaming cups of tea before the kitchen fire, usually as the night drew in.

Comforting? Oh yes, very.

Grown-up nibbles

I suppose it was inevitable that I would have little contact with the kind of things that people used to nibble with drinks. This was the era of the sherry party, which came just before the advent of the cheese-and-wine party (and the simultaneous development of the half-grapefruit stuck with cocktail sticks adorned with cubes of Mitchelstown's finest). It was also the era when people like the cast of *Mad Men* drank multiple Martinis. And that was just at lunch.

Some people did the same in Dublin in places like the Horseshoe Bar at the Shelbourne, where they would have smoked exotic cigarettes called Balkan Sobranie or State Express 555. Not Sweet Afton or Carroll's No. 1. And although I recall my father telling me about being driven around by a papal marquis in an open-top sports car, we didn't know people like that.

This is why I was only vaguely aware of cheese footballs. These little savoury spheres comprised two hollow hemi-spheres of something similar to the stuff of which ice cream cones are made. They were sealed together around a core of very salty, slightly squidgy cheese filling which, now that I have grown to man's estate, I realise must have had only a tenuous relationship with the dairy industry.

The memory sets my teeth a little on edge. They weren't very nice: the outside wasn't crisp enough, and the inside was mushy. But they still had one hell of an appeal to the pre-teens (as we were certainly not called in those days), because they were a crisps-for-adults kind of thing. Out of bounds, almost. Grown-up and sophisticated.

I remember one friend of mine speculating, aged about eight, if such dietary differences explained the fact (as we were convinced it was) that grown-ups didn't fart, while us kids were at it like trombones all the time.

There were other such snacks. Twiglets, with their splendidly savoury lick of yeast extract and kick of white pepper. And Chinese rice nibbles (which would only be seen after someone had been away). Or maybe stuffed olives: green, with a bit of red pepper sticking out.

And, of course, there would be things on Ritz crackers. A slice of hard-boiled egg, maybe, with a hint of salad cream and a final dusting of paprika. A lot of savoury things, if they moved too slowly, got dusted with paprika in those days.

It's not that we children had particularly sensitive palates. After all, we enjoyed pickles and black liquorice and industrial-strength cheese-and-onion crisps. No, it was just that some of these tastes were simply too grown-up for us. And I think our contempt for the average grown-up nibble was mingled with something like pity.

My raw infancy

When I was very small, I had a peculiar enthusiasm for minced beef. Nothing strange in that, of course, but for the fact that I enjoyed it raw. Handfuls of ruby-red raw beef stuffed into my little freckled face.

Now, I should explain that my attempts at steak tartare were both crude and nefarious. Even though nobody appeared to know about *E. coli* in those days, my mother wisely discouraged me from eating raw meat. So I had to wait for my chance and snatch a few handfuls when I could.

I still remember unwrapping the white paper that all butchers used in those days and then prising open the greaseproof package within, to reveal the object of my desire. I still remember that strange texture, the intense savouriness, the hint of blood. Oh yes, I couldn't get enough of the stuff when I was about three years old.

I wouldn't be so wildly keen now, even though I like a rare steak. It's partly the dangers of raw mince, where the pathogens that are so easily killed by heat on the surface of a piece of meat are nicely mixed in, all the way through. And also because I'm just not keen on the taste that used to appeal to me so strongly.

The finely sliced onion would be a help. As would the touch of Worcestershire sauce. But the raw egg, definitely not.

I like my eggs runny, but I've never fancied them raw. My grandfather, in his invalid years, had a raw egg in a glass of sherry every morning. I think he enjoyed the sherry more than the egg. But that's another story.

Killer instinct

Richard Mabey, the distinguished naturalist, is probably best known for his enyclopaedic *Flora Britannica*, but back in the 1970s he published a fascinating little book called *Food for Free* (which, incidentally, has never been out of print since). This is an account of all the edible things that grow wild: some are immediately delicious, others are an acquired taste.

It's a book that should be read by everyone who gets an atavistic thrill when picking blackberries on a Sunday afternoon's foray into the country. I read it as a student just before going on holiday to Mayo with a few friends. They refused to eat the sorrel soup and mushroom omelette I made, on the basis that I might poison them. On reflection, I suppose they had a point. Oh, you know, I was 99 percent sure I had found field mushrooms rather than, well, anything else. Almost thirty years later, I know a lot more about what you can eat and what you can't. And when I'm not sure, I use a book. Or better still, several books.

On a similar excursion, I bought some crabs at a pier on the coast of Kerry. They were alive, of course, and literally kicking. And they had to be cooked. After several hours in the kitchen, I produced a vast quantity of the freshest seafood I've ever cooked. But I had to eat it on my own because the companions – who believed that 'Crab Comes from Caviston's' – couldn't quite hack the preparation process and the realisation that, oddly enough, these creatures could, at one stage in their lives, actually move.

Crabs are the only creatures I've reguarly killed for the pot. OK, there was a woodcock, a disputed pheasant and a solitary rabbit, but they don't really count. (They were just desperately unlucky: I happen to be one of the worst shots in Ireland. What I really need is a sawn-off shotgun.)

I once read an article in *The Field*, a magazine in which I served as wine columnist for many years, on the best way to bag pigeon. If you go blasting away with a shotgun, you may be lucky enough to get one of the birds (probably full of shot) but its friends and relations will not hang around to let you make it a brace. The solution, of course, is to use an air rifle and a lot of camouflage. (Air rifles may sound like toys but they are not to be trifled with: they are potentially lethal to humans.) I was reminded that humans are the only pink-faced predator, so the trick is to cover up thoroughly. This will make you look like a terrorist on a training mission, so the exercise is not entirely devoid of danger.

Pick off your pigeon as it roosts in a tree towards evening. Depending on distance, it's better to aim for the head rather than the fluffily plumed body, which will absorb a lot of the impact. Again, depending on distance, you may need to allow for the wind, because the projectiles emitted by air rifles are small and relatively light. You could of course use a telescopic sight, but this is perhaps a bit unsporting. And you might well get arrested for suspicious behaviour.

Pigeons are vermin, and in areas where they are not controlled they can be a menace to anyone trying to grow vegetables, particularly cabbages and sprouts. For such gardeners, there is much pleasure in eating pigeon breast with buttered cabbage. Don't bother plucking them: just cut away the breast meat, and the feathers will come off with the skin. The rest of the carcass is not really worth the trouble. I have to say I'm not a great pigeon fancier myself. The breast meat always reminds me a little too much of liver – and that's another story.

Pigeons used to be the bane of my gardening life (and before that, magpies). Now it's rabbits. I dare say if I were a better shot and didn't worry overmuch about the fact that a .22 rifle, the anti-rabbit firearm of choice, is a high-velocity weapon, we could feed ourselves throughout the year on bunnies and have enough left over to give the neighbours rabbit pie on a regular basis.

I like rabbit. I mean, I like rabbit dead and cooked. And provided it's relatively young and fresh. A rabbit that has been hanging for a while develops a subtle aroma that reminds me of our dog. She catches rabbits, kills them, buries them in umarked graves, and, in time, exhumes them. This means that she will trot happily and affectionately into the kitchen wreathed in the smell of deceased and rather ripe rabbit. If I get a whiff of that from my rabbit pie (which is, believe me, one of the best things you can eat), I suddenly lose my appetite. At times like that, I often think that there's something to be said for an hermetically sealed urban life where all food is weighed, priced and packaged.

But not for long. There's something compelling about the idea of food for free. And that's the reason I bought Richard Mabey's book in the first place. Mind you, he enthuses about razor clams just a little too excitedly. Following his instructions for catching and cooking the beasts can be fun, but the finished product, while it does have a distinctive flavour, is uncomfortably like an industrial-grade rubber band.

Not all wild food is unconditionally delicious.

Cold curry

There are certain things which are regarded in some families as perfectly normal and natural but in others are seen as diabolical and hideous. The matter of marmalade with sausages is a case in point. This combination is a regular one in our house; its origins are disputed but some claim that they lie in attempts to cheer up school food.

We have another peculiarity in our household, and it involves curries. Nothing odd with a communal penchant for spicy food, of course. Indeed, it's one of the few meals that we all enjoy in equal measure (unlike fish, pork, many vegetables, certain pasta sauces . . .).

We take curry quite seriously and have not used a ready-made curry powder for over twenty years. Even when we get a hankering for those weird Vesta beef curries with which Johann and I grew up, we do not give in. All the spices are freshly ground.

No, nothing odd there either. Our strange secret is that we enjoy cold curry, the morning after. So great is our enthusiasm for this that we have been known to over-order from the Bombay Pantry takeaway in Glenageary so that breakfast is well taken care of.

The rationale? Well, there's something wonderful about eating a cold curry that is approaching thermonuclear spiciness. The impact is delayed, more subtle. And the texture is thicker, so much so that it can be spread on toast.

My wild youth

Organic growing was not unknown when I was growing up, but it was regarded as being a bit faddish. I was a keen gardener before I discovered an even more pressing interest in girls and stuff, and listening to Neil Young's less life-enhancing lyrics.

Every week, I'd collect my copy of *Popular Gardening* from Glynn's newsagents on Drumcondra Road and read the words of wisdom delivered by horny-handed sons of toil who looked as if they had emerged from beneath tons of earth. They didn't have much truck – as they would have have said themselves – with organic gardening.

But, of course, the organic revolution was just around the corner. This was the 1970s, and very few people realised that intensive lettuce cultivation is impossible without lots of chemical poisons to keep insect pests and fungal diseases in check. Sometimes you can actually taste the contamination. I remember the odd lettuce that tasted a bit odd, but it's been a very long time since I've consciously eaten a commercial lettuce. And anyway, the regulations are a great deal tighter now.

Organic salad is seasonal, of course. In the depths of winter, you can buy the occasional French batavian lettuce. It can be rather tough and somewhat bitter, but that can be part of the appeal. Unless you grow your own, under protection, you have no choice, of course.

Or do you? It depends how adventurous you want to be. At any time of the year, but particularly in the leaner months, you can have a salad entirely from the wild. This was something I got quite excited about in my younger days, but I have to say that my enthusiasm was not shared by my long-suffering family.

But I learned a lot in the process. Everybody knows about dandelion leaves, which are very bitter if they have not been blanched. (Just put a bucket over the plants for a week or so.) And don't forget their powerful diuretic properties. Use them sparingly, and do the same with the splendidly sharp, tangy leaves of sorrel.

Ground elder, when it's young, has a crunchy, spicy kind of taste. It's a gardener's revenge to eat this tiresomely invasive weed. You can try hairy bitter cress too – preferably the bigger plants. 'Hairy' is a relative term, by the way. I don't think most people would describe this modest bit of greenery as particularly hirsute. The taste is not so much bitter as pleasantly peppery – and, of course, it's a relation of watercress and of rocket too.

Pennywort has small, fleshy leaves which taste of very little (but when compared with a supermarket lettuce, they assume an almost fascinating flavour) and have a pleasingly succulent texture – a tiny bit like cucumber.

In May, the wild garlic or ramsons are just coming into flower. We used go to Howth Castle each year to see the rhodoendrons, but the massed ranks of garlic, and the overwhelming aroma (more sweet than garlicky, to be honest) created a much greater impression on me than the colourful shrubs which are supposed to be the Howth demesne's big attraction. Both leaves and blossoms will really pep up a wild salad (or indeed a tame one) and scent a risotto. The little bulbs do nicely in casseroles and can be put to the same use as the cultivated version.

Garlic mustard has a strongly flavoured leaf and is very common. It goes well with an equal quantity of Good King Henry – a plant that seems to grow everywhere in Ireland. But with a name like that, I don't suppose it has ever enjoyed much favour here.

It took me a very long time to pluck up the courage to pick wild watercress. There were two reasons for this. For a start, it's all too easy to confuse it for the deadly-poisonous water dropwort, and if the water source has travelled through cattle-grazing territory, you could end up with liver fluke. Which, I'm pretty sure, is not a bundle of laughs.

We now have our own source of wild watercress (the cultivated variety is quite different, and less pungent), thanks to the fact that we have our own spring and know exactly where the water has been. And I've learned to identify water dropwort with an unerring eye. Well, so far.

Common sense dictates that you don't pick your wild salad near roads (to avoid lead poisoning) or where there's a large and active rat population. (I'm driven mad by the fact that the most luscious growth of wild sorrel is on the direct path that the local rodents take when they want to feast in my compost heap.) And wherever you pick your salad, wash it very thoroughly. Wild doesn't always mean safe.

Prawn cocktail

The prawn cocktail was so emblematic of an era that the great Simon Hopkinson used it in the title of a book about the food that sustained us through the post-war years. Now, it's so retro that it's making a comeback and, as usual with these things, chefs can't resist doing 'witty' variations – which spoil the whole effect.

Let's get a few things straight. While it is not impossible to make a decent prawn cocktail from foreign prawns (the ones that are essentially big, a little rubbery and quite low on flavour), the true version is made using Dublin Bay prawns. And this is why the true prawn cocktail is rarely seen. The makings of it cost a king's ransom.

You need big, plump, juicy Dublin Bay prawns. They must be meaty, not crumbly. And they have to be fresh beyond imagining.

The rest is plain sailing. You need crisp lettuce sliced thinly with a sharp knife. This will mean that the lettuce ends up with bugger-all vitamin C left in it, but who cares? Some things are more important than mere nutrition (and there's fresh lemon juice still to come).

This bed of shreded lettuce will form a place of respose for your prawns. But first they must be coated with that pink sauce which some call Marie Rose. Why? I don't know who Marie Rose was, but I'm pretty sure she wasn't French. This pink stuff is a very British/Irish phenomenon, but it's not entirely unknown in Gallic circles.

You need mayonnaise, a little tomato ketchup, about the same amount of fresh lemon juice, a mere dash of Lea

& Perrins Worcestershire Sauce, an even merer dash of Tabasco, and finally – and optionally – a suggestion of brandy, just to fortify the whole thing.

The final flourish, of course, if you want the authentic 1960s article, is a dusting of ground paprika over the top. In those days, anything involving mayonnaise or its derivatives got such a dusting.

Growing into Guinness

Because I was just about legally entitled to buy alcohol when the alco-turkey that was Guinness Light burst upon an unsuspecting world, I am perhaps more aware than many people that the black stuff from St James's Gate is one hell of a brand.

And this, of course, is the Age of the Brand. From cars to watches, soap to computers, a vast industry creates, nurtures and monitors The Brand. In some cases, like Häagen-Dazs, the brand was created out of thin air, and very recently, but feels and looks as if it has heritage. This is the very pinnacle of marketing achievement, the kind of thing that has men with ponytails and women in severe black suits dancing for joy.

And there are other brands, the ones that have been around for decades, maybe even centuries. These are the brands that really *do* have heritage. Names like Coca-Cola, Kodak, Aga, Bentley, Michelin, and many more, have been handed down in a continuous line from the founder or inventor to the marketing manager, whose job depends on keeping sales up.

In other words, a brand that has taken centuries to evolve will inevitably end up in the hands of a few bright sparks who run the marketing department – maybe even the 'global marketing strategy development department', or whatever they want to call it.

Sometimes the brand wins, sometimes it falls victim to misguided marketing. And I fear that Ireland's most famous brand, Guinness, has become such a victim.

Guinness is so synonymous with Ireland that you could almost say that it's bigger, in brand terms, than the country.

It's ancient, by commercial standards: the first Arthur set up in business at St James's Gate in 1759, and it is much loved both by the people who drink the stuff and by those who never touch a drop. Guinness is much more than a brand; it is one of the great drinks of the world, an icon, a symbol of Irish life. Guinness is all this, and yet its fate is ultimately in the hands of the marketing people. And we should be concerned.

You see, the people who market Guinness seem to be obsessed with youth. They worry that young people won't develop a taste for the black stuff, that they will simply carry on drinking Budweiser.

So, what do they do? They take Guinness, the iconic brand, and dumb it down.

Let me explain. In the old days, Guinness drinkers served a kind of apprenticeship during which they drank Smithwick's (a much-maligned but excellent ale). In the fullness of time, the palate was able to deal with the sheer sensory assault of the taste of Guinness: the lactic acidity, the bitterness, the smokiness, the richness, almost the density of the thing.

It was a stout to conjure with, a taste that had to be acquired slowly and patiently. And, of course, in those innocent days (I went through this phase around 1980), there were fewer distractions – unless you count Harp and the early outings of Heineken. Guinness was, simply, worth it. And to some extent, it was a rite of passage, an embracing of the adult world, where pleasures were more complex but also more rewarding.

Instant gratification has done for Guinness. Now, let's nail a lie: all beers evolve over time, and the formula never remains the same. Guinness, like all other beers, and contrary to what some beer anoraks claim, has been tweaked many times in its history.

But the most recent tweaks have turned our national drink into a pale imitation of its former style, a kind of black lager aimed at palates that are too lazy, or too timid, to deal with the real thing. I never thought I'd see the day when I could say that Guinness has actually become bland. Guinness? The least bland drink you can imagine. Well, it's all relative, of course.

Tweaks in the brewing seem to have reduced the characteristic bitterness, and the acidity, always the backbone of a good pint of Guinness, seems to have been smoothened and softened. And if that's not enough, Guinness is always served way too cold these days. This policy is doubtless deliberate, in that the colder a beverage is, the less detectable taste it has. So, Guinness has been dumbed down in two respects: it has less taste than it did, and it's served in a way that reduces what taste it does have to virtually nothing.

This is a terrible thing to do to a once-great beer, one of the greatest stouts in the world and, undoubtedly, the most famous and most widely available. It is giving in to the tyranny of youth – the notion that everything from radio programmes to wine must have instant appeal for young people.

Why? Why the hell should products and services be redesigned and repackaged for people whose palates, intellects and incomes are still developing? What about the

grown-ups? If the infantilising effect of marketing contin-
ues, we will end up with a whole generation whose taste
buds stop at Liga and Ribena.

Guinness is utterly wrong for the youth market. It takes
too long to pour, it's the wrong colour (who wants black
when you can have livid blue?), it's too heavy for binge-
drinking, and even the latest version could not be described
as sweet. So why try to sell it to people who would prefer
an alcopop, or the kind of lager that makes fizzy water taste
really interesting?

Why not let them discover Guinness when they have
grown up? Why not give them something to aspire to?

Of course, I'm sure that various focus groups have
identified Guinness as an 'old man's drink'. (In fact, I know
they have.) This is the kind of thing that terrifies the living
daylights out of marketing people. Never mind the facts,
alter the perception!

The fact remains that brands which appeal to older people don't die. People get older all the time, even the young.
And however infantilised the world becomes, most of us
eventually grow up and acquire adult tastes.

The pleasures of processed cheese

It's not that we thought processed cheese was any better than the real thing. It's just that we never saw real cheese.

Growing up in the 1960s, the default cheeses were all given a helping hand by the new industry of food technology. Real cheese – and the odd bit of proper Cheddar would occasionally appear – was seriously scary stuff. It just had, well, too much flavour.

No, what we wanted was stuff that looked vaguely like cheese and which tasted rich, creamy and salty. Above all, it had to toast well, bubbling up and browning in delicious blisters above the thick slices of batch loaf.

Galtee Three Counties came in foil-wrapped triangles (and probably still does). They could be spread, in a slightly Plasticine-like fashion, on toast, which was then stuck under the grill until perfection had been reached.

There was even a selection box of triangles that purported to represent, in processed form, the great cheeses of the world. And one that certainly wasn't: a combination of onion and tomato in a shade of shocking pink. This was, for the times, very exotic stuff. Perhaps even the kind of thing that the sophisticated classes would munch at 'cheese and wine' parties, probably with cocktail cherries somewhere.

But even cheese for eating raw was processed. There was stuff called Calvita (and it may well still exist), which was so unlike any real cheese I've encountered since that its relation with, say, Cheddar was pretty much homeopathic.

The oddest such product that I can remember is Primula Cheese Spread with Shrimps. This was probably my first introduction to seafood other than fish fingers. Again, its relationship with the crustacean in question was probably fairly slight, and you could argue that it was, in theory at least, a horrendous combination. But my father and I thought it was great. Especially when spread on Ritz crackers – which added yet more salt, and a dollop of saturated fat, to the equation. And while, as I say, the spread's relationship with shrimps may have been a bit marginal, it did appear to have bits of vaguely orange stuff in it, which, we assumed, were the creature named on the box.

Primula was not an everyday comestible; it was a treat. This was for late-night suppers around the fire with plenty of strong tea. It had a faintly exotic air and it did, in a curious way, rid me of any fear of shrimps. When the time came, much later, for me to try the real thing, without any cheesy accompaniment, I munched fearlessly. I still believe that I detected a hint of those late-night suppers in the genuine article.

There were other flavours too, of course. And we tried them, from time to time. But we found that they never measured up to the original Shrimp. That would have been asking too much.

And I sometimes still hanker after toasted Three Counties, with its brown blisters still bubbling, fresh from the grill.

Salad dazed

It was the epoch before Hellmann's. It was the age of salad cream. Elizabeth David was telling people how to make a *salade Niçoise*, but the reality, for most of us, was sliced ham with tomatoes, hard-boiled eggs and some damp, often limp, leaves of a lettuce which is known to gardeners, somewhat implausibly, as Butterhead.

Yes, of course, there were variations. Cucumber was not entirely unknown, but it was generally considered to be a bit of a middle-class affectation – the kind of culinary flourish that would appeal to people who read the colour supplements such as the *Observer Magazine*.

And there was certainly beetroot. Not beetroot as grown in vegetable gardens, admittedly, but beetroot that came sliced, in glass jars, with a label that usually said 'Goodalls'. This was pickled beetroot, dark and staining, its own native flavour in a constant struggle to rise above the sea of malt vinegar in which it was packed and shipped.

I was something of a fan of beetroot. I liked the aggressive taste of the vinegar; the bonus was the way it married with equally tart salad cream to produce an effect that would take the skin off my adult palate. But it also produced the most gorgeous colour. I used to make beetroot sandwiches – which sounds likes something you would have done in Britain during World War Two.

But what, I hear you ask, was salad cream? It came in various versions. Our one was usually, like the beetroot, from Goodalls; there was a marginally posher form produced by Heinz, it being one of the original '57 Varieties', one supposes.

From a distance, it looked a little like mayonnaise, at least in colour. In texture, however, it was quite different. Where mayonnaise has a glossy, slightly jellyish character, salad cream could be poured. It was thinner than tomato ketchup, but often the bottle needed a sharp tap on its base to get the stuff flowing.

Some claim that salad cream was invented by Heinz on the eve of World War One, but there were plenty of creamy salad dressings in the repertoire of the Victorian cook. Mrs Beeton gives three recipes for 'Salad Dressing (Excellent)', each of which involves the essential base for salad cream: pounded yolks of hard-boiled eggs. And the French classic, *sauce gribiche*, which is so good with a chunky ham-hock terrine, comes out of the same tradition.

In Britain, salad cream has always been regarded as essentially working class, but it's hard to imagine any traditional manufactured, packaged sauce that is distinctly middle class or upper class. Lea & Perrins Worcestershire Sauce, perhaps. And Gentleman's Relish is not a sauce but an extraordinary combination of anchovies, salt and black pepper that is still lapped up, on buttered toast, by the relics of our own stranded gintry. But I digress.

Salad cream, as produced and marketed by Heinz, was one of the first convenience foods. Making a home-made version was simple enough, but it took time. Salad cream was reasonably cheap, and its creamy-yet-tart character made the basic salad seem a bit more exciting, a bit more glam. No wonder it was clasped to the collective bosom of the busy housewife, whether in the back-to-back terraces or the semi with all mod cons.

The argument about salad cream in class-conscious Britain goes like this. Just as Liebfraumilch and Black Forest gateau are uncomfortable reminders, for some of us, of a simpler and less pleasant time in our lives, so salad cream is forever associated with a certain bleakness that pertained before we discovered mayonnaise. It goes with cloth caps and deference and knowing your place.

Well, it doesn't really. Constance Spry, the woman who reinvigorated the art of floral decoration, may have been born in humble circumstances, but she was distinctly upper-middle class by the time she produced, with her friend Rosemary Hume, her monumental *Cookbook* in 1956. And there it is: a recipe for 'Cream Dressing (Thick)'. It goes like this:

1 level teaspoon French or English mustard
½ teaspoon salt
1 teaspoon sugar
¼ teaspoon white pepper
¼ pint evaporated milk
¼ pint olive oil
2–3 teaspoons wine vinegar

Put the seasonings into a bowl and add the milk. Mix and beat in the olive oil by degrees. Then add the vinegar gradually and adjust the seasoning. N.B.: The dressing will thicken when the vinegar is added – how quickly depends on the acidity of the vinegar.

But hang on a minute! That can't be right. It may be salad cream, of a sort, but it's just not the right *colour*. Turn the page of *The Constance Spry Cookbook* and you will find the recipe that puts paid to any notion of salad cream being a working-class condiment:

Davis's Salad-dressing

A typical English butler's dressing, and very good.

Yolk of 1–2 hard-boiled eggs
Seasoning
2 tablespoons best Lucca or olive oil
1 dessertspoon Worcestershire sauce
1 teaspoon vinegar
English made mustard to taste
2–3 spring onions, chopped finely
¾ gill single cream (approx.)

Crush the yolks well with seasoning, add the oil by degrees, then add the Worcestershire sauce, vinegar, mustard and onions. Finish with the cream; whisk or shake it thoroughly in a jar. If a thick, creamy dressing is wanted, the cream may be whipped to a froth before adding.

The period detail there, apart from the mention of a butler, is the 'Lucca or olive oil'. Lucca produces fine Tuscan olive oil. And in those days, straight 'olive oil' was what you got from the chemist to treat your earache.

I can confirm that this recipe works well. The sauce is not as thick as the stuff that comes out of a bottle, but the taste is similar. I prefer to add a bit more vinegar.

My mother occasionally made mayonnaise, but in those days – the 1960s – there was a lot of frugality about. It was wanton extravagance to use butter to make a cake, and I suppose the same went for whatever salad oil was available. So it was that mayonnaise was only produced, laboriously by hand, using a hand-beater (none of your fancy electric gizmos for my family), when there was fresh salmon.

This would be sent by a friend in the west. A fine Moy salmon would arrive every summer, and the mayonnaise would be prepared, the cucumber finely sliced, the radishes pulled from the garden and cut so they would open like little red-and-white flowers. Chives would be snipped into the potato salad, lemons would be quarted and, on occasion, a bottle of Blue Nun would be frozen to within an inch of her life.

But such events were rare. More often, a tin of Russian salad would be opened – again compliments of Heinz. This combination of potato, carrot, beetroot and peas (or am I imagining the peas?), bathed in . . . well, salad cream, actually, was a version of something that the Italians love to serve amongst the antipasti. It never quite did it for me, but Richard Corrigan's version (in his book *The Clatter of Forks and Spoons*) raises it to a new level. He serves it with smoked eel.

Nor did I like the Heinz sandwich spread about which the rest of my family was wildly enthusiastic. I think it was a kind of mayonnaise enriched with finely chopped gherkins, and maybe onion. Anyway, I didn't approve, preferring my scary combination of beetroot and salad cream – or chewing on scallions.

Chewing on scallions involved a kind of private brava-do. They were probably not any hotter in those days; my little palate was yet unblunted by years of eating weird stuff. And so, the munching of a fresh scallion involved a combination of pleasure and pain – something I would find, years later, in the consumption of chillis. I was partic-ularly taken by the potent action of the chewed scallion on the tastebuds. In most cases, the olfactory system would be knocked out completely for up to half an hour.

Using this ploy, I managed to eat certain things I

loathed. Like corned beef and sardines. Or cold rare roast beef – which I later learned to love.

We and the North Americans, with our common closeness to Elizabethan English, call spring onions 'scallions'. That's what they were originally called, and I'm rather pleased that we have held on to the proper word. They are the salad vegetable I remember with most fondness from childhood. I have a feeling that they are nowadays of no fixed abode when it comes to the modern salad.

It seems like one minute we were eating hard-boiled eggs and scallions and limp lettuce and then, suddenly, all was changed, changed utterly. Oh, I suppose it was in about 1980. A terrible beauty was not born, to be fair, but Irish salad did get more colourful.

This development coincided with the discovery of the red pepper. Soon no salad, however much it claimed to be 'green', was without its indigestible bit of rosy vegetation.

And now look at Irish salad! There's wild rocket and lollo rosso and radicchio and beet leaves and baby spinach and pea shoots and those tiny leaves that some restaurants describe as 'mesclun' and others, rather alarmingly, call 'mescalin'.

Irish salad may not be mind-altering but, despite the attempts of the average salad dressing to sabotage everything, it's probably fair to say that it's come on a bit since my First Communion tea in 1966.

On the other hand, if the raw materials are good and fresh, and you get the butler to make Constance Spry's salad cream, the traditional Irish salad makes a very happily nostalgic bit of eating.

And now I could murder a devilled egg.

Mustard

When I was still in short trousers, I served as an altar boy in the enclosed Carmelite convent on Grace Park Road in Drumcondra. Although it was only two miles from the GPO, I can remember hay being cut in its meadow and milk from its few cows being sent, by horse and cart, to other religious institutions in the area. Hampton, as it was called, was an amazing survival. Its tiny farm had never been anything else.

Every Easter, all of us altar boys would come together like a small, knobbly-kneed army to serve at the religious ceremonies. In those days, they seemed to go on for most of the day – probably because we used to rehearse before the main event.

It all culminated, in a haze of incense, with Midnight Mass, which, again in those days, started at midnight. By the time we got through the ceremony, we were tired and hungry. This was the point at which the nuns would invite us all in to their bright parlour, where the big table would be groaning beneath plates of sandwiches, serried ranks of 'iced fancies' and slices of dense, dark fruit cake. And there would be at least two vast teapots waiting to pour a scalding brew into our china cups.

The sandwiches were great, but there was a certain sense of Russian roulette to eating them. Some were anointed with mustard; others were not. But there was no way of telling just by looking at them. Occasionally, the merest hint of yellow at the edge was the warning. But usually, you had to take a chance.

The clerics who officiated didn't seem to mind the mustard – possibly having had their palates blunted by years of institutional catering – but our tender taste buds objected wildly. After all, I reasoned – somewhat unreasonably – a teaspoon of mustard in a glass of tepid water was well known to be an effective emetic! Well, so are a lot of things.

I had been put off mustard as a child because the only sort we ever had was the English version: a searingly hot, pungent and, as I thought, nasty yellow paste which would be made up as required. It took a long time for me to realise that English mustard, good as it is in certain roles, is in fact a kind of aberration.

In my teens, I used to stay with kind people in what John Betjeman called 'the conifer county of Surrey' who not only were prepared to put up with me for weeks on end but had lived in France for many years. As a result of this, they always had an earthenware jar of Pommery Meaux Mustard on the dining table. Yes, on the dining table. They meant business. This is the best mustard you can buy – it's coarse in texture and divine if assertive in flavour – but I didn't know that at the time.

I was persuaded to sniff it but I refused to taste, even though the suggestion of wine vinegar had a certain sharp attraction. I was grown up by the time I tucked into a mustardy potato salad with Toulouse sauasage and decided that this was one flavour I wanted to encounter again and again and again . . .

English mustard has its uses, of course. If you're making a cheese-flavoured béchamel sauce, a heaped teaspoon of Colman's mustard powder will redouble the cheesiness. It will also make creamed horseradish taste much more, well, horseradishy. And I've come to enjoy the merest scraping of Mr Colman's best with a slice of good cooked ham. Conversion at last. Yes, I have learned to like it. On the other hand, life without a jar of Meaux to hand is unthinkable.

It seems that the leading English manufacturer of mustard in the nineteenth century was Keen & Sons (hence 'keen as . . . ') but it was a Mrs Clements of Tewkesbury, the mustard capital of England, who discovered how to dry the interior of the mustard seed so that, when milled, it came out as powder rather than as an oily smudge.

The significance of this is huge. If you mill fresh, as distinct from fully dried, mustard seed, the pungency of its flavour will peak within minutes and then decline rapidly. This process can be arrested by the addition of acid – vinegar or lemon juice – and thus is born any of the great European mustards. Dry mustard powder, in the English form, is in a kind of suspended animation; the addition of water transforms it into its characteristically fiery form.

It's hard to believe that Colman's English Mustard and Moutarde de Meaux are made from the same little seed – a member of the cabbage family, which grows wild in the south of England (where it was introduced by the Romans) and in parts of Ireland too.

American mustard, bright yellow and very bland in flavour, is cut with prodigious quantities of turmeric. Well, it could be worse, I suppose. And it does cut the mustard. Literally.

Parsley

Much as I love the taste and even the smell of fresh garlic, I have to say that when it lingers too long on someone else's breath, it loses its raw appeal. There are parts of France and Italy, of course, where everybody smells equally of garlic, and therefore nobody notices. That's much the way it is in our house but, as a nation, we are a long way off achieving that commendable situation.

Not a lot of people realise that parsley – ideally the flat-leaved version, and preferably the very large Italian sort – can neutralise the smell of garlic if you chew a few sprigs thoroughly before swallowing. I don't know if the French devised their *persillade* with this in mind, but its combination of garlic and parsley, both finely chopped, is an essential in many dishes.

The Italians go further and add the finely diced rind of a lemon to make *gremolata*, but I don't think the citrus element does anything to suppress the pungency of the garlic. It is, however, an essential accompaniment to osso bucco, the slow-cooked slice of shin veal which often goes with risotto *milanese* (or vice versa). It's also simply lovely on pasta or sprinkled on grilled meat and, in a curious way, makes parsley taste even better than usual.

In the British Isles, we have tended to favour the curly form of parsley, largely because it is quite decorative. We are less likely to eat parsley than our Continental neighbours, and more likely to use it as a disposable garnish – which seems a shame. Butchers' shops used to account for huge amounts of curly parsley (the variety is called 'Moss

Curled', by the way) but now they use artificial green plastic stuff that fools nobody.

Parsley sauce – a white béchamel liberally fortified with chopped curly parsley – is probably the commonest use for the stuff, and almost obligatory with boiled bacon in Ireland. I refused to eat this as a child. Indeed, I refused the bacon too. But once I made my own parsley sauce, I was an instant convert.

The Italians believe, quite rightly, that the best flavour is in the stalks; they grow giant cultivars which can be cooked rather like celery. Hamburg parsley produces parsley-flavoured roots about the size of a slender carrot; when cooked, they taste quite like celeriac – which is, of course, a close relative, along with celery. But to be honest, it's not one of the world's great unsung vegetable heroes. True, it's easy to grow, but you will need a good, rich soil if you want to avoid getting thin, stringy roots.

Food is often the subject of snobbery, and parsley is no exception: the curly-leaved sort is looked down upon by the kind of people who slavishly collect beautiful cookbooks with pictures of terracotta-coloured Tuscan kitchens. Yes, the flavour is different, but I don't think it's significantly weaker. When deep-fried, it keeps its shape and the colour deepens – a further point in its favour. I have to admit that I'd always favour the Italian flat-leaf version myself: it's easier to grow and there is just so much of it when it does come up.

Coming up – or germinating – is something at which parsley is generally supposed to be slow, and some gardeners pour boiling water over the seeds. Actually, parsley comes up in its own good time. I find that it rarely hangs about for more than a fortnight, and it does like a little heat, so use your kitchen window ledge.

There really is no point in buying parsley, because it grows luxuriantly all year round and will withstand even the coldest weather. Actually, I have a theory that parsley tastes best in the depths of winter, but that may be because it has such a green, fresh, vegetal taste, and this is the time of year when we crave such things most.

Parsley is a biennial. That means that its life cycle extends over two years: it will flower and run to seed in the second summer. You can keep on top of this by sowing parsley each spring and disposing of the plants once they have flowered.

Blaa, blah, blaah

Anyone who grew up in Waterford will know about – let's settle on one spelling – the blah. And the same goes for the former boarders at Newtown, the Quaker school in the town. They have brought memories of the blah with them all over the world.

I came late to blahs: when I was in my teens, my sister moved to Waterford and introduced me to this strangely named bread item. So strangely named, indeed, that I thought at first it was what her small children had decided to call them.

We are talking about what in other places might be called a bap or even a soft burger bun (for which purpose the blah serves remarkably well). But the typical blah is given a very generous shake of flour just before baking. This has a tendency to fall off as soon as you pick one up, and it inevitably makes you feel as though you have emerged from, if not exactly a snowstorm, then at least a wintry flurry.

Blahs are made from the same kind of white yeast dough as batch loaves, but their history, it is said, is rather different. Huguenot settlers, who arrived in Waterford from France in the late seventeenth century, brought with them a kind of economical croissant which was made from leftover bread dough. This they called a 'blaad'.

How like a croissant it actually was in the early days, we will never know. Perhaps the dough was rolled thinly and interleaved with a lot of butter. That would amount to a rough approximation of a croissant.

However, Regina Sexton, the food historian, says that Edmund Rice, founder of the Christian Brothers, used to feed the poor of Waterford with blahs. It seems unlikely that these would have had a high butter content: butter has always been a bit of a luxury.

The thing to remember about your blah, apart from the risk of being sprinkled with flour before you eat it, is that they don't keep. They are best eaten on the morning of purchase, or popped in the freezer.

The art of the picnic

There's a photograph of me celebrating my fifteenth birthday way back in May 1974. I can't remember where it was taken, but I'm pretty sure it was somewhere in County Wicklow. And the small glass in my hand undoubtedly contained a measure of Harvey's Bristol Cream: Heather liked to launch her celebrated picnics with a certain civilised style.

Heather became my unofficial godmother during my early teens, shortly after she and her mother, both Scottish Presbyterians, had made firms friends with my Irish Catholic parents. Heather was for many years private secretary to the brilliant but eccentric Sir Basil Goulding, a small but distinguished-looking man who used to travel to board meetings of the Bank of Ireland on his trusty roller skates. Otherwise, he drove one of the very few Porsches in Dublin. Heather, and her friend Amy Laidlaw, eventually retired and moved to Connemara, where they ran a bed-and-breakfast establishment that was noted for its warmth and both the quality and the quantity of the food.

Heather's approach to picnics was, to me and my family, revolutionary. When I was about nine, my parents, my uncle Desmond and I travelled to many of Ireland's most famous national monuments: the Rock of Cashel, Monasterboice, Glendalough, Clonmacnoise and others. The deal was that my uncle would provide the transport for us, a car-less family, and my mother would deal with the sustenance.

We would leave for far-flung ruined abbeys or Norman

castles early on a Saturday with a basket filled with foil-wrapped sandwiches: ham mainly; egg frequently; chicken less so, as it was a bit of a luxury in those days. Sometimes there would be tomato sandwiches. (I can appreciate a tomato sandwich when it is freshly made, but its loses all its appeal after the tomatoes' considerable moisture has escaped into the bread and you end up holding a pink, sodden mass that threatens to disintegrate into your lap.) Occasionally there would be a true treat: the cold sausage sandwich, the lunch of champions; a solid slab of sustenance which, anticipating some of the elements of fusion cuisine by decades, formed a rather magical combination with Club Orange, the fizzy drink with 'bits' of orange suspended in it. Oh yes, that was the way to build yourself up for the afternoon, for climbing up round tours and for perching precariously over medieval precipices (this was before the concept of health and safety had been devised: my uncle's car didn't even have seat belts) and taking in great lungfuls (OK, smallish lungfuls: I was only nine at the time) of country air.

Our antiquarian picnics provided a fine feed, but my mother's deft touch in the kitchen tended to abandon her when it came to picnics. Maybe it was because she had been a Girl Guide in her teens that she saw the portable sandwich as a kind of potential life-saver rather than a meal. Her sandwiches did what sandwiches were meant to do, and no more.

Heather, on the other hand, understood that the picnic was an art form. She deconstructed the whole thing (not that anyone consciously deconstructed anything in those days) and started from scratch. She asked herself why we had to slum it just because we were out of doors, and she was a stickler for the minutest detail.

Her picnics would start with a sherry, carefully poured into immaculately polished Waterford glasses. And then there would be soup, very often *potage Crécy*, a glorious combination of carrots and cream: the carrots in this soup bore no resemblance to the ones you got in stews.

After that, there was what nowadays would fall under the broad category of charcuterie. There would be proper ham, carved off the bone and packed carefully so that it would lose none of its moisture. And various salami – a foodstuff which was quite exotic for those days, especially the one that shamelessly advertised itself as being flavoured with garlic. And coleslaw on the side.

To be honest, I had never seen either coleslaw or salami until I was invited, aged twelve, to lunch at a school friend's. It was all a bit overwhelming, especially as they had just moved into a vast castle in County Meath and I had never seen, let alone eaten, stuff like this before. When I was asked if I wanted more coleslaw, I said yes, not knowing whether I was going to get the meaty-roll thing or the creamy, crunchy stuff.

Three years later, and here I was eating them, in the open air, celebrating my fifteeth birthday, still a little giddy after the small glass of sherry which somehow marked the start of my transition to the grown-up world. And there were crunchy bread rolls, and *proper* linen napkins, and King's Pattern cutlery, and a cake. (Heather was a prodigious baker.) And there was jelly, not as a nod to my juvenile status but because Heather, always so considerate and kind, knew that my father loved the stuff.

It was a good lesson to learn so early: that picnics can be as simple or as grand as you like, and that there's something rather special about trekking off to a special place and opening up the basket. It doesn't have to be Glyndebourne. In fact, having other people picknicking alongside you is distracting and can descend into a kind of competitiveness. Picnics demand privacy – unless you are on the beach, in which case a decent distance is enough.

A bottle of white wine or decent beer that has been chilled in a rapidly moving stream tastes better than if it has come out of the fridge – but it does take time. And if the season is on the cusp of autumn, there is no dessert quite as good as freshly gathered plump blackberries: they taste of the countryside and have the added benefit of being both delicious and *free*. The thing about the picnic is that it's not the same as eating alfresco. Or camping, for that matter. It's a very distinctive form of eating and drinking.

I think we should have moved beyond the vacuum flask at this stage. Tea and coffee from these containers, which were once considered to be almost-miraculous devices, never tastes quite right. True, the flavour is not so much like liquid plastic as it was when I used to take a flask to national school (and invariably break it, this costing more than the convenience was worth). But keeping tea or coffee warm for hours on end does nothing for either beverage.

What you need is a kettle – the sort that can be powered from the car or put on a gas ring. Or the clever one you can buy in camping stores: this has a hollow centre in which you kindle a small fire, and you get boiling water in no time.

Freshly brewed tea or coffee makes a picnic a feast. Isn't it strange how the simplest things, done properly, can elevate something from the utterly mundane? I quite fancy the idea of the glass of sherry too. Though these days it would be a good, dry *fino*, not one of the sweet ones. But each to his own.

There are times when a mug of tea and a cold sausage sandwich, with a view, and good company, are as good as a feast.

Tinned salmon

I'm not sure when I last saw a tin of salmon. This is strange, because I was brought up on Picnic and John West. Well, maybe not *brought up* on it. But my youthful diet certainly featured a lot of this kind of pink stuff.

I was fond of tinned salmon – which is as different from the fresh stuff as foie gras is from Petit Filou. Even more different, indeed, than fresh tuna is from the tinned kind.

The thing that struck me about tinned salmon as a child was that the bones, most noticeably the vertebrae, were rendered soft and eatable by the canning process. I can still remember the soft crunch, and how it was slightly off-putting.

My mother used to make a terrific tinned-salmon pie. I must try to recreate it some day. She mixed the flaked salmon with chopped hard-boiled eggs and sliced scallions, then encased the mixture in buttery rough-puff pastry. It was lovely. The thought of it now brings me back to Sunday evenings long ago.

The sauce of division

I don't know if it's a particularly Irish thing to define your-self, or the group to which you belong, by what you *don't* do, rather than what you do do. If you see what I mean.

Growing up, I was vaguely aware that you imbibe social attititudes by a kind of osmosis, and that what seems per-fectly natural and rational to me and mine might be utterly bizarre to others.

Much was said about your family by the newspaper that you 'took' – and in those days, if People Like Us bought the *Evening Press* or the *Evening Herald*, it was seen as a bit of a betrayal of the middle classes. Mind you, my family's late adoption of television (it arrived when I was well into primary school) was probably based on the idea that the new medium was aimed at 'the masses'.

Food was involved too. People Like Us didn't buy Shipham's Meat Paste (much to my disappointment, when I first came across it in a friend's house). Nor did we have much truck with sliced pan. And the strange thing is that while pickles were kosher, if I may borrow a phrase, brown sauce was absolutely beyond the pale.

This meant that we never, ever had YR or HP Sauce in the house. And it also means that I had never tasted the stuff until I sat down to write this passage. I had a deprived childhood.

YR Sauce, when I was little, came in an angular bottle with, as far as I can remember, a design on the label that looked a bit like the willow pattern you get on china. It was, and still is, made by Goodall's not far from where I lived as a child. It was proudly Irish, even if the YR stood for 'Yorkshire Relish'.

Now, Yorkshire Relish was a thin brown sauce, not unlike Worcestershire sauce in appearance, and it too was, and is, made by Goodall's. The original of the species was made by a company called Goodall Backhouse. They appear to have been the first to produce a commercial version of the relish, in Leeds, in the 1870s.

Nowadays, the Yorkshire Relish baton, so to speak, has passed to Henderson's of Sheffield, whose orange livery makes their bottles look – to me at any rate – rather like Lea & Perrins Worcestershire Sauce.

Anyway, the YR Sauce that was never put on our table was, as far as I can gather, a kind of thick version of Yorkshire Relish. It tastes similar, even if it's distinctly sweeter.

Its great rival was HP Sauce from England, the initials standing for the 'Houses of Parliament'. The picture of the Palace of Westminster made it look terribly respectable. At least that's what I thought. Even though HP never featured at home, I had a feeling that it might have been a superior kind of product. I didn't know, at the time, that the then British prime minister, Harold Wilson, was much given to drowning his dinner in the stuff.

HP is superficially similar to YR, but there's a bit more substance to it, a little more fruitiness and spiciness in the flavour, and it's a little less sweet. But to be honest, I wouldn't thank you for either. And of course, both the YR and HP brands have been diversified, so you can get all sorts of variations on the theme, if you are so inclined.

They have their fans, of course, and YR is something of

a cult product amongst the competitive barbecuers of the United States. I'm not at all sure that this is a recommendation.

Another brown substance was regarded – although this was never said out loud – as being rather infra dig. This was Branston Pickle – which I later learned to enjoy with cheese and crackers. Maybe it was a colour thing. There was no problem with pearly white pickled onions or bright yellow piccalilli, and I assaulted my young palate regularly with both.

Chutney was definitely within the pale, even the commercially produced mango version from Sharwood's. And there was one called Major Grey's. But chutney was approved, I reckon, because most of it was home-made and there was a respectable Protestant ring to it. Home-made chutney suggested a commendably thrifty spirit. Long before the notion of sustainability was ever talked about, gluts of home-grown fruit and vegetables were preserved for future use in a form so piquant and sharp that it needed laying down, like a wine, for a few months before it was ready to be spread on cold meat or slices of cheese.

And the raw materials didn't matter a great deal. The fact is that once you use enough salt, vinegar and spice, and there's sufficient boiling involved, you can make chutney out of anything. Even old shoes.

Lea & Perrins

We always had a bottle of Lea & Perrins Worcestershire Sauce, with its distinctive orange-and-black label, in the kitchen cupboard. It was a standby for my mother when she made – as she did all the time – soups and stews and casseroles.

It has a very strong flavour, and whenever I encounter it, it induces a warm sense of nostalgia – probably because it formed part of those soups and what-have-you that fortified me when I got in from school. During my student days, one of the staples in my repertoire was tinned tomato soup (usually Heinz) with a great deal of Lea & Perrins shaken in before serving.

There are other versions, but the original recipe is Lea & Perrins. The story goes that Mr Lea and Mr Perrins, two chemists in the town of Worcester, were asked by some local grandee to make up a very potent spice mix, the recipe for which had been brought back from India.

In or around 1838, it struck the two chemists that this pungent mix might be converted into a sauce with commercial possibilities. They mixed it with vinegar, and for good measure – history doesn't relate why – threw in some anchovies too. Perhaps they were thinking of the fermented fish sauce which was a feature of cookery in ancient Rome, and which was not unlike *nam pla* from Thailand.

Whatever the reason, the resulting brew was horrendous. The barrel in which it had been mixed was put to the back of the cellar and, so the story goes, forgotten. A few years later, it was discovered, and the potent liquid tasted. It was clear that it had lost its fiery edge and was now fit for human consumption. By the early 1840s, Lea & Perrins Worcestershire Sauce was rapidly becoming one of the first food brands in these islands. The company has been through many owners but is now in the hands of Heinz. The sauce is still made from the original recipe – and is still produced in the town of Worcester.

Lea & Perrins Worcestershire Sauce, I later discovered, is an essential ingredient in a proper Bloody Mary and is also de rigueur with Welsh rarebit, especially if you're having it as a savoury after dinner. I add a dash to Irish stew, and it's not unknown for me to use just a suspicion of it in a *ragu* – the Italian meat sauce that goes so well with spaghetti. The trick is to use very little, so that you can't actually taste the Lea & Perrins in the finished sauce. It needs to hover in the background, working its magic.

Marmite

One of the reasons why Ian McKellen gave such a magisterial performance as Gandalf in *The Lord of Rings* may have been the availability of Marmite in even the remotest reaches of New Zealand. It seems that he forgot to pack his usual supply and was mightily relieved when he discovered that he was not going to be Marmite-less on location. He probably dreaded having to make do with the rather anaemic antipodean version which is known as Vegemite.

When the iconic Marmite brand celebrated its centenary a few years ago, its advertising campaign was possibly the most honest in the business. 'You either like it, or you hate it,' proclaimed the strap-line, and this is undoubtedly true. In fact, Marmite has always been promoted in a way that acknowledges its very divisiveness. This is clever marketing, because the suggestion is that Marmite-fanciers are, in some sense, the elect. There has even been a limited-edition Marmite, made with Champagne. It does taste different – but not different enough for those who have not been converted to the cause.

I have a theory that you have to be introduced to Marmite early in childhood in order to overlook the, er . . . somewhat off-putting appearance. It does look like tar. In fact, it looks like the stuff you get when you blow cigarette smoke through a tissue. Anyway, I missed out on Marmite in childhood and have, until fairly recently, approached it with somewhat less enthusiasm than is the hallmark of the true aficionado.

Before I was converted – and I will admit to having the

convert's zeal – I once produced toast and Marmite for my wife, who was sick in bed at the time. Apparently I lathered the Marmite on in quanties that would have floored even the most ardent enthusiast. This reminds me of how my virtually teetotal parents would pour half-pints of whiskey for horrified guests. Marmite is something you need to understand from personal experience.

Marmite has a very strong, very intense taste. And it's salty almost beyond belief. There's nothing subtle about its near-manic savouriness, and it has the curious quality of tasting very meaty while being strictly vegetarian. If not used subtly, it will, like so many commercial sauces made in Ireland and Britain, swamp the flavour of any food with which it is put. It's all about understanding how to use it to best effect.

Despite my late conversion to Marmite, I was not left without yeast extract (for that is what Marmite is, for all its mythic status) in childhood, because my patriotic mother bought an Irish product instead. It was called GYE (*qv*).

Marmite does indeed divide opinion very sharply and, although I don't have any figures for this, I suspect that the Marmite-haters significantly outnumber the Marmite-lovers. Marmite-lovers, like all minorities, are slightly touched by fanaticism, and those that have a sense of the history of the stuff revere the memory of Baron von Liebig (he of the condenser that we all used, with some trepidation, in science lessons at school), who discovered or invented (or even isolated, I don't know) yeast extract in the 1870s. In its basic form, of course, it's a by-product of the brewing process, but the Baron managed to turn it into something that is, arguably at least, palatable and useful.

Before he worked his chemical magic, spent yeast was always fed to cattle. And the cattle were probably very happy about it. The fact that most spent yeast from breweries still takes this route is something that doubtless upsets Marmite enthusiasts.

For some unknown reason, it never caught on in von Liebig's native Germany, but the process was adopted by the Marmite company, which was set up in Burton-on-Trent, the famous brewing town in Britain, in 1902. A decade later, sales were considerably boosted when vitamins were discovered and their role in nutrition explained. Marmite is packed with B-vitamins, and these days is fortified further with folic acid. Marmite (the word means 'an old-fashioned cooking pot' in French) was perhaps one of the first so-called 'functional foods'.

Thinly spread on white toast is my favourite application for the stuff. But it's also remarkably good when mixed with dry mustard powder and spread on the fat of a joint of beef before roasting. It's an essential addition to what I call 'brown mince', a kind of Bolognese without the tomato, on which many of us were brought up. Its name, and its label, suggest a role in cooking rather than as a foodstuff in itself.

I have always detected greater enthusiasm for Marmite in the Protestant population than in the majority in Ireland, which may explain its modest status in the national larder. The biggest jar of Marmite is not sold in Ireland, nor can you buy such delicacies as Marmite-flavoured crisps here. But Twiglets, a crunchy snack that combines yeast extract and a great deal of white pepper, for so long confined to the United Kingdom, are now on sale in Tesco.

Garlic

Looking back on it now, I'm suprised Monica Sheridan wasn't had up for heresy when she spoke in favour of garlic in the early 1960s. Monica was our first television cook, and she got into trouble for licking her fingers on screen. (This was well before Nigella Lawson made such behaviour not just acceptable, but sexy.) Domestic-science teachers very nearly took to the streets.

There was a feeling in those days – and I know this only by hearsay, as I still had my full complement of milk teeth at the time – that fancy food led to immorality. Garlic, it was known, was in daily use in France, and we all knew what the French were like.

No, what we wanted in those days, it seems, was Good Plain Food – a phrase which was always spoken with implied capital letters at the start of each word. And that meant meat, potatoes and a couple of vegetables boiled into total submission. And absolutely no foreign filth like garlic.

To be fair, I think it was largely Irish men who were to blame for this. They dreaded any experimentation in the kitchen because it disturbed what John Charles McQuaid described, in a different context, as 'the tranquillity of their lives'. Actually, he was talking about Vatican II.

When I was growing up, my late mother was, I suspect, the only person I knew who heeded Monica's clarion call in relation to garlic. I'm not sure that she really liked it very much, but she certainly felt that some dishes were better with it. I have a notion that she also had some belief in its therapeutic qualities.

She first came into direct contact with garlic in the south of France in the early 1950s, when she took a donkey ride in the foothills of the Pyrenees and her guide amazed her by munching his way through a whole bulb of the new season's harvest. The smell, she always recalled, was 'like nothing on earth'. Garlic fiend that I am, I can well believe it.

If you can't beat them, of course, you have to join them. If you consume prodigious quantities of garlic yourself, you will never notice it on the breath of others. And not just on the breath. Allicin, the key component of garlic, is so potent that it will make its way through your pores and add a certain something to the atmosphere.

There are still quite a few people who disdain this magical bulb, and not all of them are confined to these islands and North America. In India, there is a very strict religious sect known as the Jains who are forbidden not only from engaging in agriculture because they might harm living things in the process (you bet they might) but also from eating members of the onion tribe.

Historically, aristocratic and priestly groups have always looked askance at garlic (and leeks, come to think of it) because, presumably, they were considered rude, crude, barbaric. The fact that I'm particularly keen on both of these members of the allium tribe seems to underline the fact that I've never been keen on the priestly or the elite.

In late April, you will see the flower heads of wild garlic appear in the hedgerows. In milder parts of the country, the brilliant little white stars will burst into bloom by the middle of the month; in colder areas, they will wait until May before they perfume (or pollute, depending on your point of view) the spring air with a sweet garlic fragrance.

Not many people know that you can use this common wild plant in cooking – not just the slender bulb, which you will find a couple of inches below the surface of the soil, but also the spear-shaped leaves. The tiny white flowers are great in a salad. John Seymour said that 'good food is unthinkable without onions', and I agree. But I have to say that for me, the same applies to garlic.

If you've ever tried chewing raw garlic – and I have – you will know that it packs a weighty punch. You pop the skinned clove into your mouth and, yes, there's that distinctive aroma, but nothing alarming. Then you bite and, for a moment, nothing happens. You chew a little, and suddenly your mouth is on fire. It's not so much an overwhelming taste, more a sensation: fiery, spicy, hot, bordering on the painful.

Mindful of the fact that you need to chew the garlic in order to release its beneficial compounds, you steel yourself for the ordeal and masticate frantically, trying to get it all over and done with as soon as is consistent with what garlic fiends regard as 'best practice'. And then you swallow.

If you've been in the habit of chewing raw garlic for some time, swallowing will deliver a warming sensation as the stuff slips down. Novices will just get heartburn.

The after-effects are well known. Raw garlic is a great deal more pungent than the cooked sort, and both the taste and the smell linger on the breath. But it goes beyond that. Once the stuff has been digested, some of the more fragrant compounds are expelled through the lungs and the sweat glands. So even when the garlic is coasting through the gut, it scents the whole body.

Just as smokers never notice how the stench of cigarettes clings to their clothes, hair and breath, so is the garlic fiend unconscious of the aura that constantly surrounds them. The more you chew, the more pungent you become, but you will be unaware of it – at least until people start to recoil at your approach.

So why do people do it? Of all the herbs, spices and so-called superfoods, garlic occupies a distinguished place. It has antibiotic and antifungal properties, and is said to reduce LDL cholesterol (although this is disputed). It also makes the blood less prone to clotting, by reducing platelet stickiness and making the blood flow more smoothly. So much so, in fact, that people who eat a lot of garlic are advised to knock it off a fortnight before elective surgery.

I know this from personal experience, as someone who takes a garlic supplement (not the raw stuff) every day. A few years ago, a phlebotomist withdrew his needle from my arm after taking a blood sample. Before he could stick a bit of cotton wool over the tiny puncture, it started to spout like Moby Dick. 'Oh my God!' he said. 'You should have told me you're on warfarin.'

Hence the plethora of garlic capsules, tablets and potions on the market – some of them, heaven forfend, 'deodorised'. Some people would argue that if you can't take the smell, you don't deserve the benefit. I'm not so sure. In my view, the most pleasant way to eat raw garlic is in the form of pesto: here it is ground with fresh basil leaves and pine nuts, then mixed with olive oil and Parmesan. (Strictly speaking, it should be pecorino, but I'm a Parmesan man myself.) Tossed with pasta, this is one of the best things you can eat, in every sense.

Grilled rustic bread rubbed with raw garlic (so that the garlic grates itself into the rough surface) and drizzled with olive oil (which *does* help reduce LDL cholesterol) is easier, and almost as good.

The Japanese have developed a clever compromise. They use a special ageing process for garlic which reduces the smell while retaining much of the active compounds. This version is available in tablet form as kyolic garlic. It's certainly a more discreet way of taking large quantities of this remarkable herb, but, as I know from personal experience, you can grow addicted to the pungent power of the raw bulb.

Guggy

Smell is the most evocative of the senses. And the most comforting smells for me include the aroma of flannel pyjamas warming on the fireguard, Lifebuoy soap, white pepper and hot butter. No, there's nothing kinky about the list. It just happens to be the stuff of my early childhood.

White pepper and hot butter formed an essential presence in one of my favourite meals when I was very little. This was a soft-boiled egg mashed up with a fork in a teacup. (My mother loved pepper, and I'm very grateful that she introduced me to it so early.) And the butter? Well, is it decent to expect anyone, child or grown-up, to consume an egg without butter? Absolutely not. I mean, can you even begin to *conceive* of egg with margarine? Or dairy spread? Pah!

In my fairly literal-minded household, a boiled egg mashed up in a cup was known as 'boiled egg mashed up in a cup'. But many of my contemporaries recall this delicacy of infancy as 'guggy'. Some of them called eggs 'gugs', which makes sense. It's easier to make that sound when you are still adjacent to the potty-training stage.

The spelling varies because, no doubt, very few of us have ever had cause to write it down. My informants refer, also, to 'googy' and 'gougie'. One of them called it 'goofy', but something tells me this was a typo. I'm told that eggs which fail to hatch are known, in Limerick, as 'gogglers'.

I suppose the reason that guggy – let's agree on that spelling – was invented was because very little people find it hard to tackle an egg in a shell. Inserting a teaspoon into a small hole and lifting out the semi-liquid contents is quite a task when you're, say, three years old.

Of course, we all graduate to boiled eggs, and we rejoice when we hit the dizzying heights of sophistication represented by the eggcup. A little later – probably about ten minutes – we discover the pleasure of inverting the empty eggshell and inviting an unsuspecting parent to eat it. This is possibly our first experience of the pratfall gag.

Anyway, boiled eggs, toast and marmalade remain a comfort in early life – or at least they do for me – because of their simplicity, their deliciousness, and their ability to connect you with a time when life was a lot less complex, and possibly much more exciting.

A poached egg is, by contrast, a rather grown-up dish. I don't know why, but us kids didn't get them – in either sense. Now that I am of riper years, I can't get enough of them. A very fresh, free-range egg from one of the neighbours, cracked into a saucer, slid into simmering water (no salt, no vinegar) and allowed to just set, then drained and placed on hot buttered white toast. A pinch of salt and a grind of pepper. There is nothing quite like the molten yolk of such an egg as it soaks into the toast underneath. This is my grown-up guggy.

The hard-boiled egg, of course, is a different animal altogether. During my childhood, it had a different role: in the making of egg sandwiches. When I was very young – about six or seven – my school sandwiches seem to have been strictly vegetarian. The only fillings I can recall are banana and egg – though mercifully not both together.

Banana is a frightful thing to put in a small child's sandwich. They go brown and slimy and, if nicely ripe, will pungently scent a school bag for months on end. But egg sandwiches! It has taken me many years to recover from the horrors of the ones with which I was sent to pre-school.

The eggs would become more and more sulphurous as the morning wore on. When, at last, the sandwiches were liberated from their foil wrapping, the whole room would be enveloped in a stench created not just by my lunch but by those of the other unfortunates whose mammies had decided to fortify them in a similar fashion. There was general agreement that the smell of egg sandwiches and farts had a lot in common. As it happens, there's a scientific basis to this: what they have in common is sulphur.

Mind you, most of us grew up, to some extent, on hard-boiled eggs. Not to the same extent as our northern European neighbours, all of whom seem to start the day on cold hard-boiled eggs (always white, rather than our pre-ferred brown), ham and bread rolls.

No, as I say, we had them in our school lunches, in fleshed-out salads and in one of those delicacies of the 1970s, the Scotch egg. This take on the hard-boiled egg – an egg encased in sausage meat with an overcoat of crisp breadcrumbs – was popularised by the *Hamlyn All Colour Cookbook*, without which no middle-class kitchen, with its brown and orange curtains, was complete.

A cold Scotch egg makes a fine lunch, but it's much better eaten hot. Although Scotch eggs became part of my teenage repertoire in the kitchen, I never managed to get the egg perfectly centred. I still can't, to be honest – though I get less practice these days.

Coddle

Coddle doesn't look very appetising. And, to be honest, when you consider what goes into it, and how it's cooked, most people will not be slavering at the thought of tucking in.

But that's the great thing about this dish, which sustained the poor of Dublin for cenuries in one form or another. It is, like so many wonderful dishes, much more than the sum of its parts.

Having been delicately nurtured amongst the middle classes of the capital, I was well into my twenties before coddle crossed my path. And I was surprised by how much it appealed to me.

This combination of sliced rashers, sausages, onion, potato, parsley (if you're lucky) and white pepper is simply brought to the boil and allowed to simmer, whereupon it emits a beguiling scent that stimulates the gastric juices like nobody's business. So much so, indeed, that when you remove the lid (it takes about thirty minutes to cook), you are so hungry that even the sight of pink, fatty things floating in an off-white (sometimes distressingly grey) broth does nothing to blunt the appetite. In that sense, coddle is a miracle.

It has the advantage of being a one-pot meal. You just throw all the ingredients in, add some seasoning, cover with water, and off you go. Traditionally it not only fed large, hungry families for little money but also ameliorated the effects of what is traditionally known as a 'rake of pints' (of Guinness) in much the same way as crubeens did.

You rarely see coddle on sale, doubtless because of its lack of prettiness. I can't imagine how you could make it look better. Some misguided folk insist on browning the sausages – which is a terrible solecism. The texture of the sausage is changed, and your coddle is then not a true coddle. At home, we rely on fistfuls of finely chopped parsley thrown in at the end. This is not traditional – the parsley is supposed to go in at the start of the cooking process – but we like to think that we are operating within the true tradition of Dublin coddle-makers. I suspect that many readers are yet to encounter coddle. I would urge them to make that leap. Even if they spoon it up with their eyes closed (which can be quite a messy business).

McDonald's

The gastro-snobs – those people who prefer to put status symbols on their plates rather than food – were sent into a state of shock a few years ago. One of their great heroes had admitted that he quite likes McDonald's.

Ferran Adrià is probably the most famous chef in the world. His El Bulli restaurant – a shrine to Adrià's unique style of high-tech cuisine, which has been dubbed 'molecular gastronomy' – had what you might call the hottest tables in the world. Before he closed the restaurant's doors in 2009, 2 million people a year tried to eat there – which meant that you had a 1 in 400 chance of getting a booking. Heston Blumenthal (of snail porridge and bacon-and-egg ice cream fame) is probably his best-known disciple.

When Adrià speaks, foodies everywhere listen. And his enthusiasm for the world's biggest purveyor of hamburgers is bound to put the cat among the pigeons. He admits that he has eaten there on only a handful of occasions (he's a very busy man, obviously), but he did say that he wanted to go back.

McDonald's must be pleased, especially after the bruising it received from, amongst others, Morgan Spurlock, whose film *Super Size Me* became a surprise hit. The documentary, which appeared in 2004, argued that McDonald's were profiting from the epidemic in obesity, and detailed Spurlock's physical decline as he spent weeks eating food solely from the fast-food chain.

Well, no surprise there then. We all know that eating nothing but fast food is bad for you. Around the same time, a New York judge threw out a case brought by an overweight man who was seeking damages from McDonald's for – you're way ahead of me here – making him fat. The case was reported in the *New York Times* under the memorable heading 'Hamburgers Make You Fat. No Kidding, Rules Judge'.

Now, strange as it may seem, I really enjoy an occasional trip to McDonald's. I will go further and say that I quite relish the taste of the chain's signature dish – for want of a better term – the famous Big Mac. It is not as other hamburgers, I agree, but its combination of minced Irish beef, bun, salad, pickles (ah yes, those pickles!) and weird but curiously moreish mayonnaise-based sauce is damn good. The Quarter Pounder with Cheese is more in the classic hamburger tradition, and provides the only acceptable use for those slices of processed dairy produce known, generically, as Easi-Singles.

And the fries? Well, the fries are unique to McDonald's. My only problem is the lack of consistency. When they are good (i.e. very fresh, crisp and not over-salted), they are very good indeed. When they are flaccid, they are, frankly, crap. And you would have thought that McDonald's, with their University of bleedin' Hamburgerology, could get on top of that problem.

The first McDonald's in Ireland opened the year I left school, in 1977, and during that summer I consumed a considerable number of cheeseburgers in that seminal Grafton Street branch. But I had first eaten in a McDonald's somewhere in Germany when I was about fourteen. It was, I thought, quite breathtakingly sophisticated, and I genuinely believed the food was very tasty. I fell in love, at first chew, with dill pickles – a taste which I now seem to share with nobody at all of my acquaintance. Ireland, at that point, seemed far too dreary and depressed to provide the soil in which a McDonald's culture could thrive. Well, it *was* 1977.

How Anthony Bourdain, the *enfant terrible* of American chefs, can accuse McDonald's of blandness beats me. Bland? Come on, Tony! You may not like the taste of a Big Mac, you may in fact be revolted by the very idea of eating one, but it's certainly not bland.

My own feeling is that most food writers are afraid to say what they really think about McDonald's, i.e. that in their heart of hearts they quite like it. Some of them, no doubt, deliberately combine their own very creditable enthusiasm for local and artisan food with a completely unrealistic notion of what people actually like to eat. It is certainly not fashionable amongst the food-critic confraternity to admit to stepping inside the doors of what is the most popular 'restaurant' chain in the world.

An exception to this rule, as to so many others, is Michael Winner, who reviewed his local McDonald's for the *Sunday Times*. He found the Quarter Pounder with Cheese 'average' and the buns 'squashy' (he doesn't understand that this is how they are meant to be) but declared that a Chicken Legend would be acceptable 'in any upper-class restaurant'. (Good as it is, I'm not sure it would fit the bill at Guilbaud's.) He also mentioned that McDonald's serves Vittel mineral water while diners at the uber-posh Scotts of Mayfair have to make do with an inferior brand. Bravo! He opined that his Quarter Pounder with Cheese was not a patch on the one at the Ivy, and I've no doubt he's right. But he didn't mention the difference in price.

While the reluctance of food writers to deal with

McDonald's in anything but the sniffiest tones suggests a considerable degree of insecurity (a quality to which the egregious Mr Winner has been a stranger since birth), I wonder about the snobbery of those punters who shriek in histrionic horror at the mere mention of the double arches.

Well, in my view, it's like homophobia (albeit a lot less serious in terms of its consequences). Those who protest most loudly about the 'junk food' at McDonald's are probably those who dream about it, fantasise about the milk shakes (the charms of which are elusive to me) and fetishise those long, stringy 'French fries' which everybody else calls chips.

And yes, of course, there is a great deal of hypocrisy. I am always amazed at what food snobs are prepared to eat (and how much they are prepared to pay). They will think nothing of eating a dull, pedestrian meal, based on industrial-grade ingredients, served with a large side of pretension and condescension, provided it's dished up in something approximating a restaurant.

And yet they would not dream of eating a hamburger in McDonald's – a burger made from very carefully sourced grass-fed Irish beef, prepared with hygiene standards that go well beyond the requirements of the FSAI. And for a fraction of what they will pay in any number of less choosy and less well-run establishments.

A huge number of people who disapprove of McDonald's serve their kids convenience foods at home that contain stuff which would never even be considered for inclusion in a Big Mac. And McDonald's serve salt-reduced ketchup. How many parents do that?

Of course, McDonald's is far from perfect. There is evidence that their reliance on South American beef in some markets is indirectly leading to destruction of the rainforest. And it's only since *Super Size Me* appeared that they began to provide proper nutritional information about their products – and dropped the Super Size promotions.

But for a vast corporation, they are doing some good things. They have made huge reductions in packaging in recent years; they are the biggest buyer of organic milk in the UK; they are ranked amongst the Top 50 Companies To Work For in Ireland (so much for the McJob, then); and the Ronald McDonald Foundation does a great deal for children in hospital.

So, credit where it is due. McDonald's may not be a wholly philanthropic enterprise, but nor is it an evil empire. Indeed, it has changed radically in recent years, becoming much more responsive to environmental and health concerns. Its food, whether you like it or not, is sourced to very high standards and produced with much greater care than in other fast-food outlets. And it's a very significant customer for Irish beef.

It's not a place to eat in every day; McDonald's is best as an occasional indulgence. They do what they do very well, and very seriously. I don't see what there is not to like.

Oh, the pickles? Yes, I know they divide opinion pretty sharply, but I happen to be very fond of them. And for all I know, Ferran Adrià may be planning to turn them into an ice cream, if El Bulli opens again.

Veg in restaurants

Ireland, for some reason I don't understand, harbours a visceral hatred of two things which I greatly like: trees and vegetables. Trees are forever being condemned as unsafe and as hazards to traffic. Any excuse will do, it seems, to call in the tree butchers.

With vegetables, it's a little more subtle, but the process is particularly noticeable in restaurants. I don't suppose it's entirely true to say that the heart automatically sinks at the sight of a kidney dish filled with a combination of carrot, calabrese, potato, mangetout and cauliflower, but it's certainly not a cheery sight. You see, there is a rule in the freemasonry of Irish chefs that it is an indictable offence to serve vegetables others than those listed above. Just as it is to serve a salad which comprises only green lettuce.

Apparently, minor sins are forgiven. Such as serving French beans, provided – and I stress – that they are out of season and overcooked. A ratatouille is permissible, but only if mushy, produced with too much tomato and made with really crap raw materials. Otherwise, it's immediate expulsion from the hallowed halls of the chefs' grand lodge, to say nothing of the nameless horrors that are then inflicted on the black sheep.

If a chef is really asking for it, he or she should dish up vegetables which are (a) fresh, (b) organically grown, (c) barely cooked and (d) interesting. A chef who serves scorzonera, salsify or sea kale is likely to be disemboweled. (Just as well Richard Corrigan works in London.) Courgettes are borderline, but they must be overgrown, flavourless and, ideally, out of season. If there is any question of serving them in June, when they are the size of your little finger, possibly with the flower still attached, and sweated in a little butter, the boys are sent round.

A dispensation to serve cabbage may be obtained provided it is cooked long and hard and – this cannot be stressed too much – kept warm for many hours in a bain-marie. On no account must it be simply steamed, then tossed with butter, a few cubes of crisp bacon and a sprinkling of pepper. Heaven knows what agonies John Howard must have suffered; this was a great favourite at his Le Coq Hardi.

Root vegetables such as beetroot, celeriac and parsnip are banned outright, and carrots, although actively encouraged, must not be served within three months of harvesting. Otherwise it's impossible to achieve the right degree of woodiness.

Jerusalem artichokes, globe artichokes and cardoons are punishable by a slow death. You can see how effective this injunction is. When did you last see one on an Irish menu?

The higher officers of the chefs' grand lodge are allowed a few indulgences. I can tell you of just one. They are permitted to use frozen baby sweetcorn, in combination with mangetout, to produce what is known to them alone as a 'stir fry'. Some things are better left untouched.

Parsnips

I reckon that an opinion poll would identify parsnips as our least-favourite vegetable. Maybe Bord Bía have already established this through extensive market research but are keeping it quiet for fear of upsetting the powerful parsnip lobby.

Hundreds of acres must be devoted to growing the things, and thousands of square metres of supermarket space is devoted to displaying them. Yet nobody seems to eat them. This is, to put it mildly, a bit weird. Especially when you consider the law of the conservation of matter and all that kind of thing.

Fine words butter no parsnips. This old saying implies not only that parsnips need to be tarted up, but that parsnips, at root, so to speak, are pretty unpalatable. I grew up in a parsnip-free household (I think the odd one made it into soup mixtures), so I came to this root vegetable with no experience and not much enthusiasm.

I am now a convert but will admit that the only way I eat them is roasted. Being a naturally sweet vegetable, they caramelise nicely in a roasting tin and compliment any meat. I'm not sure I'd fancy them on their own, but I expect they could be good tossed with coriander, parsley, garlic and a generous squeeze of lemon juice. As well as being sweet, they have a mildly spicy kind of flavour. Not spicy as in curry, more spicy as in Christmas pudding. And, odd as it may seem, I've actually quite enjoyed a parsnip-and-orange dessert that involved a lot of bitter dark chocolate. But that was not something thrown together by me, perish the very thought. It was the fruit of the considerable labours of a very fine chef.

Parsnips are very easy to grow, but for most gardeners the problem lies in the fact that they occupy the ground for most of the year. I usually sow mine in early March and pull the first one not long after the first frost. It may seem like old wives' lore, but parsnips taste much better after they have been subjected to very low temperatures. Before the frost, they seem to have a kind of bland soapiness to them, but you can put them in the freezer for a few hours. Don't let them freeze solid, but a good frosting will help the floury starches convert into the sweet sugars that make a parsnip, for what it's worth, a parsnip.

My parsnips stay in the ground until the spring for the simple reason that this is the best way to keep them fresh, and further exposure to frost will make them taste even better. Exposure to rats and slugs is a lot less beneficial, but this has rarely been a problem. Rats, in theory, should be very keen on parsnips, as they have a very sweet tooth. In the past, they tucked into the sugar-beet crop, but these days they will probably try any sweet root they can lay their paws on. You parsnip-growers have been warned.

The first parsnip of the last season was a joy to dig – the better part of a foot long, big, fat and pretty straight. The next four were stumpy. The roots had delved down three inches, hit the notorious stoniness of our soil and divided every which way. I can't tell you how frustrating this is – and it's impossible to calculate how many of the rest have suffered a similar fate. But they still taste good.

The keenest parsnip-growers avoid any trouble with stones by taking a crowbar and making a parsnip-shaped hole in the ground, then filling it with potting compost and sowing the seed at the top. I did this once; so successful was it that I had to *excavate* the almost yard-long parsnips that resulted, rather than merely digging them up. The vegetable garden looked like a cross between *CSI* and *Time Team*.

Parsnips are prone to canker. This is usually not a major problem: it inflicts superficial damage around the top. However, commercial growers use preventative chemical treatments, so, as always, try to buy the organically produced version. You may just find you like them.

And if you do decide to grow your own, bear in mind that most normal households will struggle to get through a dozen of them in a year. And share the seeds with friends and neighbours. They won't keep until next year, and the average packet could feed the whole of our island nation.

Gravy

In 2003, when I was helping clear out my parents' house before it was sold, I came across a bottle of Goodall's gravy browning. It was almost full, not a little dusty, and on the side there was a little sticker (which would have been cutting-edge stuff in retailing at the time it was applied) which read '1/9d'. That's not old money. It's old, old money, in which there were twelve pennies in a shilling and twenty shillings in a pound.

In other words, my mother's gravy browning dated from before the introduction of decmial currency in 1971. And I know, as it happens, that it was acquired well before then. I'd hazard a guess that it had been in the kitchen since about 1968.

My mother was a great gravy-maker, hence the fact that her bottle of gravy browning – what possessed her to buy it in the first place? – was barely touched in more than forty years. She had the knack of ensuring that enough of the juices from the roast would brown sufficiently in the pan to produce gravy of exactly the right hue.

Mind you, at Christmas she would make stock from the turkey giblets and then use this to make the gravy – something that never appealed to the offal-hater in me. That was the only version of her gravy that I approached with less than gusto.

We had Oxo at home but I never saw it being used. And I have a vague recollection of a packet of Bisto towards the back of the cupboard, but, again, I can't recall seeing it being wielded over the roasting tin.

Our gravy was made in the simplest of ways – and it's the method I still use today. The caramelised juices and the crusty bits in the roasting tin are dissolved with some boiling water or stock; there is much stirring and scraping; and then this lovely, brown liquid gets thickened with a cornflour or arrowroot solution and seasoned, before going to the table.

Nowadays, there might be an occasional twist. Like deglazing the pan with some white wine or adding a dash of soy sauce, for both colour and savouriness. But the essentials of good gravy remain the same, timeless, changeless. It's just the quality of the average piece of meat that seems to be deteriorating.

Oxo

I'm sure there are people in white coats who have worked tirelessly on this kind of project for months, if not years – but the Oxo boffins cut notches out of the traditional Oxo cube, so that it now looks like a very squared-off 'X'. The dimensions remain the same and – this is the clever bit – so does the weight. How did they do this?

Well, the new Oxo cube is more tightly compressed. It's that simple. But it does seem odd that the rationale behind the morphing of Oxo was, according to the manufacturers, to make the cubes more easy to crumble.

It seems that the 'X' shape gives more grip, more purchase, for the fingers that are doing the crumbling. And then they go and compress it more – which presumably makes it less easy to crumble. Oh, I give up.

Actually, I never took up Oxo in the first place. I have a vague memory of there having been a packet in the larder at home when I was a teenager, and I may have crumbled the odd cube into an alleged spaghetti Bolognese in a university garret, but I didn't establish a relationship with the stuff. I have a feeling that my mother regarded Oxo with some disdain: the kind of thing that might be useful in a gravy emergency (as distinct from a grave emergency) but certainly not something that would feature in her repertoire of ingredients.

Bisto, however, was quite beyond the pale. I think it may have been the legacy of the cheery urchins known to generations as the Bisto Kids. The problem was – and I'm only guessing here – that the loveable, cheeky Bisto Kids seemed to come from the wrong end of the, er . . . socioeconomic spectrum. Oxo was a bit common; Bisto was unthinkable.

Norman Tebbit, one of the grandees of the Tory Party, and someone who is now making a name for himself as an enthusiastic cook (I swear, I am not making this up), reacted to the news of the remodelling of the Oxo cube with the words 'Is nothing sacred?' Which, oddly enough, is exactly what I said.

And then I thought: '*Sacred?* How sacred can Oxo be?' It's true that the newly reshaped cubes do actually contain some extract of beef, but there's a lot of other stuff in there too, like monosodium glutamate, and caramel, and a great deal of salt. It's not the sort of thing that I'd like to crumble into anything I'd be planning on eating.

Oxo came about because of the Liebig technique for producing beef extract, one of the many triumphs of nineteenth-century chemistry. At first, the beef extract was a thick liquid, not unlike Bovril today. Oxo was developed shortly before World War One as a cheaper version in order to expand the market.

Curiously enough, Oxo's brand career has been quite different from its contemporaries – and rivals, in some respects – Bovril and Marmite. This must surely be because it has a brilliant brand name: the strength of the Ox, an added 'O', and you have a three-letter palindrome that lends itself to bold images.

Just look at photographs of Dublin during World War One, and you will see posters with the word 'OXO' leaping out of the streetscape, still a potent brand symbol after all these years. In a sense, Oxo suffered because it's name was so good.

Bovril – the first syllable is, of course, for 'bovine' – is not nearly as clever a name. So the advertisers had to work harder. One of the great early posters showed a mournful-looking ox inspecting a jar of Bovril with the slogan: 'Alas, my poor brother.'

During the mad-cow scare in the UK, Bovril dropped beef from the contents and replaced it with yeast extract. There was an outrage and, after the EU ended restrictions on the import of British beef, Bovril returned to its original formula.

If Oxo dropped the beef, I'm not sure that many people would notice. And I'm morally certain that there would be no outrage, no campaigns or petitions.

You see, Oxo is not loved in anything like the way Marmite and Bovril are. The 'Oxo family' in the TV commercials of the 1980s did their best to give the brand a personality, but I don't think it worked.

I am assured that you can actually drink the stuff, but somehow it doesn't seem appropriate. You certainly can't spread it on your toast – well, not very evenly or neatly, at any rate. So its role is confined to the kitchen, where it serves to enhance the flavour of whatever mum (or occasionally dad) is cooking – which it does not through its inherent beefiness but because it delivers a hefty dose of monosodium glutamate.

Yes, it's a stock cube in a sense, but not the sort that anyone is likely to use to make a risotto. Its main function appears to be in the making of gravy. And for a lot of people, making decent gravy remains the Holy Grail. In fact, nothing could be easier.

You simply pour the excess fat off your roasting tray,

pour in a little water, put it over the heat and scrape away at the crusty bits in order to dissolve their goodness into the liquid. Then add a little salt and pepper and thicken, if you wish, with some cornflour.

There will always be a role for Oxo, of course. For a start, a brand as potent as this will take a very long time to fade. A new shape is just an excuse to draw attention to Oxo, and it has been highly successful in this. And as more and more people spend less time in the kitchen, it would seem that Oxo-assisted gravy will go on and on.

But something tells me that it will never be a Bovril or a Marmite. You can't endow a brand with loveability by changing the shape of the product. Nor passionate customer loyalty, for that matter.

But at least it gives some of us the pleasure of asking the rhetorical question: 'Is nothing sacred?'

Hazlett

My father had certain favourite foods. Lamb cutlets with thickly buttered slices of batch loaf, for example. And Toblerone. And the occasional bit of toasted cheese.

But the oddest was hazlett. Or possibly 'hazlitt'. Or even 'haslet'. There seems to be little agreement on how to spell it. Anyway, what we are talking about is, essentially, a kind of meat loaf made from pork (or at least bits of the pig) and breadcrumbs. It was sliced thinly and served cold with salad. You can still occasionally get hold of it.

The origin seems to be English, and 'haslet' is well known in Lincolnshire and some of the northern counties. It sounds much the same: a blend of chopped or mixed pig's innards such as lungs and kidneys, and even, in some old recipes, the windpipe with breadcrumbs, pepper and sage. The word 'hazlett' seems to be derived from the Latin *hasta*, meaning 'sword', and referring, in this instance, to a piece of meat ready for roasting (presumably on something sharp) in front of the fire. How we ended up calling our version of it in Ireland after an eighteenth-century English essayist, William Hazlitt, is just one of those mysteries.

As I recall hazlett in Ireland, particularly from Saturday lunch at St Columba's College, Rathfarnham, in the 1980s, it was quite smooth-textured and tasted of sausage meat and a great deal of white pepper. Unusually, it had little flecks of what I assume was red pepper running through it. Had I known about the traditional recipes, I might have approached it with a bit more circumspection, I suppose.

But I would have missed out – even if hazlett was considered exciting only in rather drab and difficult times.

If you have never tried it, and think it sounds like just a variation on white pudding, it's not. The ingredients may be similar, but the texture and the taste are quite distinct. A fine foil for a good, sharp chutney or some bright yellow piccalilli.

Pepper

A few years ago, I was very surprised to find myself in agreement with a member of the late Bush administration. I have to say that Ambassador Thomas P. Foley, as he prepared to leave Dublin, hit the nail on the head in one respect.

Mr Foley was, in my book, as wrong as wrong can be on many issues, including genetic engineering, but he's right about pepper. Yes, pepper. It may seem an odd topic for him to dwell on before he bade farewell to the grey skies of the Emerald Isle, but he pointed out that the general run of pepper in Ireland is not up to snuff (not that anyone should trying using it as snuff, of course).

Being a diplomat, of course, he put it differently. He commented to the effect that pepper tastes different in Ireland than back home. What he meant was that pepper in Ireland is only woejous.

Now, me being something of a pepper aficionado, this comment caught my attention and I concluded that (a) broadly speaking, Mr Foley is right, but also that (b) he must eat in very good restaurants back home. Because there's a lot of really rubbish pepper available to the citizens of the United States, provided they stay out of the better restaurants and delis of San Francisco and New York.

To be honest, if I may digress very slightly for a moment, I felt that Mr Foley should probably have drawn a discreet veil over his pepper problems, because if he thinks, for a moment, that an American with a well-tuned palate will pine after proper pepper while on assignment to Dublin, just imagine what it's like for us Irish having to drink what the Americans insist on calling 'coffee'. (Once, while attending a conference in the US, I switched the 'Coffee' and 'Hot water' labels and nobody appeared to notice.)

But back to the pepper problem. Pepper may be one of the oldest spices in the world, it may have been a form of currency in the ancient past, civilisations may have been built upon it, fortunes made and lost with it, but we came to it rather late in this country.

I entered the 1960s as a babe-in-arms and left it having just graduated to long trousers. And during all that time, I seem to recall that my mother got through only a handful of medium-sized tins of ground white pepper in the kitchen cupboard. It was used sparingly, but at least it was used.

Even the freshest white pepper is not much to write home about. By the time my voice was threatening to break, we had entered the 1970s, and I discovered real pepper. I was staying with rather sophisticated relatives in England, and I caught a whiff of the fruity fragrance of freshly ground black pepper. I was seduced. But I managed to embarass myself by trying to shake the pepper from the top of the grinder. A quick lesson from my kind hostess meant that I had morphed, as far as I was concerned, from a northside gouger with bum fluff into something resembling a Parisian *boulevardier*.

On my return to Dublin, I suggested that the family should acquire one of these devices. My father and I ran one to earth in Smith's of the Green, now long gone. I still treasure my original 1972-model pepper grinder.

True pepper is the berry of a plant called *Piper nigrum*, which is a native of India's Malabar coast. These days, it's grown throughout the tropical world, and most of the planet's pepper is traded through Singapore. But the best pepper still comes from the Malabar coast, and the best of that is known as the Tallicherry. It delivers warmth and fragrance, not fieriness.

But what of the different shades of pepper? Well, black peppercorns are the unripe berries that grow on the pepper tree – not so much a tree, actually, as a very vigorous vine that can grow three metres high and scrambles over the other tropical plants. They are picked and dried in the sun, and the pulp between the skin and the seed shrinks, producing the characteristic hard, wrinkly surface.

If you let the peppers ripen fully, they turn bright red and the outer skin peels away (with a bit of help) to reveal the seed itself. This is white pepper, which is generally thought to be too ripe to have much flavour of its own, and which is not highly prized.

Then you have pink peppercorns, which are harvested just as the outer skin of the berry starts to turn colour. These are rare and should not be confused with 'red peppercorns', which are not pepper at all but the berries of a South American shrub which smell and taste vaguely pepperlike. Green peppercorns, which have become very fashionable in recent years, are merely unripe pepper berries which are either dried or pickled. They have a very distinctive taste (and can make a great steak sauce if used with some cream to deglaze the pan). The lemony-tasting Sichuan peppercorns come from an Asian cousin of our own ash tree and, again, have nothing to do with the true pepper.

Ireland's only dedicated spice merchant is Arun Kapil of Green Saffron in Midleton, County Cork. He imports all of his pepper from an uncle in Kerala and is planning a plantation there to grow the ultimate pepper.

'The spice trade is controlled by the huge companies,' he explains. 'When they buy pepper, they want a very low moisture content, because that way their stock won't lose value in their warehouses. It's not the way to get good pepper. The best peppercorns are plump, and they have an amazing scent. Crush them, and you have a perfume that will fill the whole room.'

No wonder it has been called the black gold of India. When the king of the Visigoths took Rome in 408 AD, part of the ransom he demanded was three thousand pounds of pepper (the rest was five thousand pounds of gold).

This stuff clearly bore no resemblance to the flecky sawdust that passes for pepper in Ireland these days. When did you last dip some bread in good olive oil and then sprinkle it with cracked pepper and inhale the ripe, round, warm aroma and go 'Wow'? Probably when you were in Italy.

It's interesting to think that Indian cuisine depended on pepper for its spicy heat for thousands of years before that American interloper, the chilli, arrived. And pepper has a different kind of heat: rounder, deeper, more complex. Chilli, to be honest, is a bit brash; its heat lacks breeding.

But pepper, the ubiquitous spice, is taken for granted. Ambassador Foley is right. In Ireland, the quality of pepper runs the gamut from A to C. Not A to Zee.

Freshly ground or crushed pepper (and it has to be fresh) can transform a humble soft-boiled egg or a dollop of goat's cheese on a cracker. Smoked salmon is unthinkable without it. Would you even consider putting a piece of meat in the oven without first anointing it with pepper? A grilled mushroom is only half a mushroom without it.

Civilised life would be very difficult without garlic. It would be no bed of roses in the absence of decent coffee. The world would be a much poorer place without anchovies. And proper croissants with apricot jam.

But civilised life without pepper? Quite impossible.

Asparagus

It's a strange thought – and I hope some readers at least are too young to remember it – but there was a time when asparagus was rare and a bit posh, and actually rather intimidating. It's a bit like smoked salmon in that respect. When I was doing my Inter Cert, way back in 1975, smoked salmon was consumed mainly by members of the Jewish community, and asparagus . . . well, asparagus was eaten mainly by the people who grew it themselves. This was not the kind of veg you got in Quinnsworth in those days (where the range was confined – and I don't think I'm imagining this – to swedes, carrots and cabbages; oh, and spuds, of course).

You might be forgiven for thinking that asparagus is a native, like Paddington Bear, of Peru. Virtually every stick of the stuff seems to come from there, and it's available all the time, with no regard to the calendar. Indeed, it's a fair bet that very few people know when this noble vegetable is in season.

Well, the answer is May and June: if you want to avoid the Peruvian perennial, that's the time to leap upon the green spears, as I do each year, with glad cries. For a few weeks, we can enjoy the best asparagus in the world, as grown in Ireland and England. Either, as God intended, dipped in melted butter which has been sharpened with a few drops of lemon juice, or devilishly, decadently, with hollandaise sauce – the stuff that so many people are too scared make.

It's not just the freshness, or the lack of air miles. I think it has something to do with the climate here in Ireland and in England, where it's cool and the growth is slow. This vegetable develops an intensity which is rivalled, I think, only by the fresh peas which come in as the asparagus fades and the spears turn into ferns.

People can be a bit chauvinistic about Irish and English asparagus. They are a little dismissive about the white asparagus which the Europeans adore. Well, I love both. The white sort tastes quite different. It has a complex, minerally taste, with a touch of bitterness. Even pickled, it's gorgeous.

The Dutch and Germans love white asparagus. They have a particular way with it, serving it very simply, with melted butter and a scrape of nutmeg. Now, we don't think of nutmeg with vegetables: it's just not in our cookery tradition. But it's worth trying.

White asparagus is basically the same vegetable but it's grown differently. It's kept in the dark – usually by drawing up the earth around the spears – and this blanching process imparts its unique flavour.

Green asparagus grows in the open air and in full light but, being a spring vegetable, it's at the mercy of weather. Fine weather can provide a good crop, especially in the sunny south-east. We don't grow a lot of asparagus commercially here, but Wexford is the Irish asparagus capital. Unfortunately, most of the asparagus bought here comes from France or England.

You can buy asparagus 'crowns' in the garden centres. You plant them by spreading out the roots two or three inches below the surface of the soil; the soil needs to be rich in organic matter and free of weeds. Don't harvest any spears the following year, and take only one or two spears from each plant the next year. Allow the asparagus fern to grow over the summer: this builds up the plant's strength. Cut it back in the late autumn, when it's gone brown and dry. A well-kept secret is the fact that asparagus is very easy – and cheap – to grow from seed.

Prepare green asparagus by trimming the spears and peeling away any tough skin towards the bottom. (The peelings and trimming can go into soup.) Steam until *just* done: you want to keep a little bite. Serve either with melted butter and some shavings of Parmesan or with hollandaise sauce.

Asparagus can kill many wines but pungent Sauvignon Blanc, especially the New Zealand kind, puts up a good fight. The perfect partner is a Savennières from the Loire valley.

Hollandaise Sauce
(to be served with asparagus; enough for six people)

225g butter
1 tbsp white wine
2 tbsp white-wine vinegar
2 egg yolks
Salt and cayenne pepper
Lemon juice, if needed

Start by clarifying the butter. Melt it in a small pan, then very gently pour off the golden oil, leaving the milky residue behind (which you then discard).

Put the wine and vinegar into a non-reactive pan and bring to the boil. Turn down the heat and and allow to reduce until only a tablespoon is left in the pan. Remove from the heat.

Allow to cool for about a minute and then stir in the egg yolks. Slowly pour in the clarified butter, whisking all the time, until all the butter has been absorbed and the sauce has thickened.

Taste and season with salt and a little cayenne. If you feel that the sauce needs more acidity, add some lemon juice.

Pour the hollandaise into a sauce boat and keep in a warm place until the asparagus is ready to serve.

By the way, the reason why we are inundated with asparagus all year round is thanks to the bungling of the US government. Some years ago, they decided to discourage the Peruvians from growing cocaine by encouraging them to grow asparagus. They failed to do their homework, however, and didn't twig that asparagus likes sandy coastal soils, while cocaine thrives in mountainous regions: the whole exercise was a complete failure. And the US destroyed its own asparagus industry, which had thrived in Washington State for almost two centuries.

Strange stuff, asparagus. It not only makes your pee smell weird, it also confuses the CIA. What a vegetable.

Smash

I've no idea what Cadbury's were doing messing around with vegetables, but the fact is that they invented instant mashed potato in the 1970s. I have a theory that it was because they knew that cold mashed potato can be used to make a particularly moist and arguably delicious chocolate cake (I swear this is true), but somehow I don't think the Bournville boffins were thinking along these lines.

Anyway, the fact is that Cadbury's produced a form of powder which could be poured into a bowl, followed by the prescribed amount of hot water, and then whisked with a fork, thus creating a substance which many people, especially those who suffered from short-sightedness and challenged taste buds, claimed was indistinguishable from mashed potato.

Was? What am I saying? Smash is still on sale, and there are even generic versions of it. The brand, which is now owned by Premier Foods, initially languished, possibly because way back in the 1960s there was still a sufficient work ethic to ensure that the peeling and boiling of potatoes was not regarded as an undignified and essentially wasted slog.

It took one of the most memorable TV advertising campaigns of the twentieth century (for so it has been voted, if you don't believe me) to pitch Smash into the big time. The commercial involved a bunch of rather cute Martians having a giggle at the poor little humanoids, who still cooked potatoes from scratch. It's not the kind of advertising that would work these days, but in 1974 it took the world (well, Britain and Ireland) by storm.

So much so, indeed, that even my mother tried it. And knowing her, she probably fortified it with so much butter and black pepper that wallpaper paste (which Smash somewhat resembled) would have been passably palatable.

Even Smash fans had to admit that the product was not without its flaws. Small pockets of the powder would pop up in the midst of the mixture and, ah – how shall I put this? – spoil the effect.

The last time I ate Smash was in a school dining hall in the mid-1980s. And I didn't like it very much at all, as it happens.

GYE

I was in my late thirties before I embraced (a rather sticky business) the black, viscous stuff which was invented by Baron von Liebig and is now known as Marmite. And when I wrote about this on my Megabites blog, I mentioned that while I was a stranger to Marmite as a child, I was familiar with a not-dissimilar substance called GYE. (Note the capitals: they stood for Guinness Yeast Exract.) I mentioned that GYE had gone off the market just around the time I was learning to sleep through the night – but I was wrong.

GYE survived until 1968, the year in which I celebrated my ninth birthday. It had been launched in the 1920s, when one of the team of scientists at the St James's Gate brewery, a Dr Millar, developed his own technique for creating an extract from the spent yeast, which had previously been added to animal feed.

The extract, named GYE for obvious reasons, was launched in 1927. Demand was such that a new, purpose-built plant was created within the brewery; this plant could produce a quarter of a ton of GYE every day. That is a lot of black, tarry, very intensely flavoured stuff. It would cover a vast acreage of toast.

But GYE was to become even more popular. Within two years, production rose to a ton a day. By 1950, the plant was producing twelve tons of GYE every week.

'Some bright crystals sometimes form in the extract from time to time. These are phosphates and therefore valuable as food', stated a GYE leaflet from the 1930s. It's hard to imagine a marketing department going with that line these days.

I always think of GYE as coming in a little round jar with a label in dark blue and cream (which were the traditional colours of the St James's Gate brewery until Diageo decided to change to black and gold). However, the promotional literature I've seen for GYE uses cream and red. It must be my memory playing tricks again.

I saw and held a jar of GYE – actually, it's mainly phosphate crystals at this stage – only a couple of years ago. It was a rare privilege. This sacred jar is carefully secreted in a house in the south of England, where it is treasured by Arthur Guinness's great-great-great-great-great-great-granddaughter. As it could well be the last jar of GYE in existence, she has no intention of opening it.

Not long before GYE went off the market, it featured in a biscuit created by Jacob's, of Cream Cracker fame. Essentially, these were Cream Crackers enriched with GYE: they had a very savoury taste and were a browner shade than the regular crackers. I think they came in a green tin. I vaguely remember eating them with considerable enthusiasm (and a lot of butter). I gather they lasted only a few months on the market: my taste, and that of the Great Irish Public at the time, don't seem to have coincided.

Denny's pies

Despite the Shannon Scheme and all that carry-on, Ireland was not great at embracing technology when I was small. I once tried to phone Dublin from Ballinskellings, County Kerry, in 1981, only to be asked, with a sigh, by the operator if it was a matter of life and death. Matters of life and death got priority on the creaking, hand-knitted, steam-powered telephone system of the time.

True, there was television, and that required quite a lot of technology, especially in the orientation of the 'bunny's ears' to maximise reception and reduce the snowstorm effect. And in the latter half of the 1960s, Dublin and Cork got buses – follow me closely here – with remotely controlled concertina-type doors. When I saw my first one, I was almost overcome with the whole, well, *modernity* of the thing.

We were used to America having technology. Anyone who read the *National Geographic* could see that. All those labour-saving devices like fridges and washing machines and – oh, the decadence – dishwashers. And even across the water in England, they had stuff like motorways, and that Post Office Tower with the revolving bit on top, and nuclear missiles. We had the Naas dual-carriageway, Liberty Hall and the FCA.

The English also had Caramac bars and Opal Fruits, and we were denied access to these delights. Some of us kids, especially those of us educated in the robustly nationalist, xenophobic and historically a bit misguided tradition of the Christian Brothers, probably thought this was a hangover from the Penal Laws.

Anyway, it wasn't fair. Television was full of programmes that showed vast rooms full of humming computers, the ones with the huge reel-to-reel tapes, the sort
that could now be replaced by the processor in the average
mobile phone. If you watch the original – and better – version of *The Italian Job*, you will get an idea of what I'm talking about.

Anyway, the implication was that these technological
behemoths were *everywhere* in other countries, while, as far
as we knew, there were two small ones in Ireland: serving
the needs of Aer Lingus and the ESB.

Vesta curries were, I suppose, a technological innovation. I mean, all the stuff was dehydrated, and all you did
to it was add water and simmer until . . . well, until it looked
and smelled vaguely edible. They were not terribly nice, to
be honest, but I still wanted to eat them, because this was
modern food. Cutting-edge, if you like. And a gentle introduction to spice.

But dehydration was nothing new. Erin had been drying veg down in Carlow for donkey's years, and you could
buy dried peas and carrots, and heaven knows what else.
Looking back now, I can understand the peas: freezers
were almost unknown in Ireland at the time. But carrots?
Carrots, which can be bought fresh right through the year?
I guess that didn't matter. We had the, er . . . technology,
such as it was. And so we used it. Proudly.

I mention all this as the backdrop to my discovery of
an invention which, at the time, I believed made a very
considerable contribution to the sum of human happiness.
This was Denny's steak and kidney pie *in a tin*. It was a mar-
vel. It could be stored forever at ambient temperature and,

when it was required, all you had to do was open the top, pop the whole thing into a preheated oven, and watch the pastry rise, brown and crisp. And then, inside, there was succulent beef in a rich gravy (OK, it was all relative), and . . . eeuughhhhhh! Kidneys.

I was so impressed by this invention, this march forwards, that I forgave the presence within it – the fly in the ointment, if you like – of my least favourite piece of any animal: the kidney.

I believe they still sell these tinned marvels. And I still think it's a terribly clever idea, but I haven't quite get round to revisiting the experience. I really don't want to spoil the memory.

The Captain's Table

I got converted to fish when I was in my late twenties. It was an overnight thing. There I was with my wife Johann, sitting in Trudy's of Dun Laoghaire, perusing the menu. Suddenly, I announced that I would have the plaice.

I still don't know why; it just seemed the right thing to do at the time. Maybe you just need to be ready. It was the same thing with oysters. They used to make me gag. Try as I would (and believe me, I tried), I simply could not open my throat and let one slip down. The one day, in Australia, I decided that I might give them another go. I've never looked back since.

We are not a great nation of fish-eaters, of course. As people have constantly commented, the seas off our coast were teeming with nutritious fish during the Great Famine, but even in those distressed times we don't seem to have taken to food that swims.

Sporadic attempts to make me eat fish (and thereby grow up strong and clever) took place throughout my chidlhood. They ranked with piano lessons and encouraging me to play football and develop neat handwriting in their patchy rate of success. These attempts included my poor mother creating her own fish fingers from slices of fresh haddock. The slices were marinated with oil and lemon juice and, I think, thyme, then breaded and fried until crisp. The logic was impeccable: put something that doesn't greatly appeal to a child inside an overcoat of crisp breadcrumbs, or even batter, and the crispness will win out over the contents.

I did deign to eat these little delicacies, but I never came home from school claiming that I could murder a fish finger. I wouldn't mind one now, though . . .

I didn't get real fish fingers – that is, Birdseye fish fingers – at home. Whether this was down to the fact that we had no freezer or a distaste for processed food on the part of my parents, I don't know. But I did come into contact with these funny little piscine items in friends' houses. I was never very impressed, though.

Although Clarence Birdseye, the man who invented the deep freeze for food products, patented the concept of the fish finger as long ago as 1927, the fish finger as we know it today is only a few years older than me. After some bizarre market research, in which Birdseye UK offered consumers a choice between fish fingers made from herring, on the one hand, and cod, on the other (and yes, you've guessed which fish won that contest), the frozen fish finger burst upon an unsuspecting world in 1955. Now it is apparently one of our favourite foods for children, despite issues relating to sustainability – and not just for the seriously endangered poor old cod.

So popular are fish fingers today that there are many versions on the market. However, it's worth bearing in mind that some of them contain a mere 37 percent fish. Which rather defeats the purpose, surely.

Most people whom I've asked say that the ideal accompaniment to fish fingers is tomato ketchup. I beg to differ. I think mayonnaise with extra lemon juice and some crushed garlic is yer only man with Captain Birdseye's finest. And while there's no doubt that fish – and fish fingers – do have a certain affinity for chips, I think it's hard to beat a pitta bread.

Toasted pitta filled with shredded lettuce, fish fingers and garlicky mayonnaise is a very quick and surprisingly tasty meal. In fact, I suspect that if you put it on a restaurant menu, most of the takers would be grown-ups who hanker after a suggestion of childhood comfort food.

The grown-up version of fish fingers is, of course, goujons of lemon sole. These are all very well – and 'goujon' is reassuringly French-sounding – but I think the appeal lies in how the dish reminds us of simpler, humbler meals from long ago. I mean, how many people eat goujons with ketchup as they watch television? That's the critical test, isn't it?

But what amazes me about fish fingers qua fish fingers is that those marketing geniuses at Birdseye in the 1950s seriously thought that the herring version was in with a chance of winning over the consumer. History doesn't relate if they tried fish fingers on the Scandinavians: I suspect that herring fingers might have caught on there. Accompanied, perhaps, with a shot of *akavit*?

Crubeens

They sustained us through good times and bad. They off-
set the effects of a surfeit of stout. Many of the *cailíní deasa*
owed the lustrous sheen of their hair to them. In fact, they
helped to build the nation.

And what do we do? We turn our backs on them. We're
far too sophisticated for that class of grub these days. Sure
isn't it all sea bass and linguini and lamb shanks these days?

Yes, nobody buys crubeens any more. We have lost our
taste for pigs' feet – for that is what they are – and the only
way you're likely to encounter them these days is in restaurants where the chef is prepared to spend hours transform-
ing them into something that looks a great deal more
acceptable in polite society.

It's a shame, because crubeens are packed with flavour
and goodness if they're cooked carefully. They are also as
cheap as chips. Cheaper, actually. The most I've ever paid
for a pig's foot is €1.50, and I'm told you can get them for
as little as fifty cent if you shop around.

Crubeens were the food of the poor and, in that sense,
they belong to a great European tradition of dishes that
come out of having to make do. Crubeens belong to an age
when waste was considered a sin.

Mind you, most butchers will react with either puzzle-
ment or a sense of nostalgia if you ask for crubeens. They
haven't seen them for years, just like the rest of us. It has
been chefs who have kept up a – very modest – demand for
them, but not because they want to put them on the table.
The water in which you cook your crubeens, you see, is

transformed into the most wonderful, dense, thick jelly.

There are two kinds of crubeen: the cured and the fresh. The cured version has simply been put through the bacon process; what little actual meat lies within will be pink. The fresh one remains, essentially, pork.

The crubeen's image problem starts on the outside. There is no ambiguity about what it is. It's, well . . . a hoof, of a sort. Almost, dare I say it, a paw. Put like this, a fillet steak is just a very expensive slice of meat; a crubeen is a bit of anatomy.

Then there's the hair issue. Many pigs' feet will come complete with some bristles; these, needless to say, have to go before you get cooking. Hugh Fearnley-Whittingstall, who is a keen fan of the trotter (as they call them across the water), advises shaving. This conjures up a picture of anointing the crubeen with shaving foam and delicately plying an old-fashioned cut-throat razor.

No. Far better to do what chefs do: take a blowlamp to the crubeen, and any hirsute problems will vanish in a puff of smoke.

Now you need to cook your crubeens for a long time in a lot of water. So, fill a large pot and put in some roughly chopped onion, carrot and celery. Throw in a bay leaf or two and, if you have it, a few sprigs of thyme. Pop in your crubeens and bring to the boil, then turn down the heat and let it simmer for about three hours, or until very tender.

Chefs usually wrap each crubeen tightly in muslin before cooking because they want to keep the shape; otherwise, they do tend to fall apart – but this is how they were traditionally served. There would be a big pile of slippery, steaming pigs' trotters, along with plenty of soda bread and butter and a pot of mustard, at the end of a long evening in the pub.

Yes, the cooked crubeen, au naturel, so to speak, is not a thing of great beauty. There is very little meat in there, just a few sweet morsels. And there are a lot of small bones, which are best removed before you get on to the eating. But the bulk of your crubeen is a mass of white wobbly stuff with something like the consistency of jelly, and a very fine taste.

Now, a lot of people, in their innocence, think that this is fat. Fat? How much fat is there in a foot? Especially an animal's foot. This is tough connective tissue broken down, through long, slow cooking, into edible form. And it adheres to the skin, which, like any pork skin, has the ability to crisp up in a very delicious way.

I'll confess that I wouldn't be mad keen to tackle, if you like, a naked crubeen. I prefer them tarted up a bit. For example, having taken out the bones and opened up the crubeen so that it's flat, I spread some smooth mustard on the interior side and then sprinkle on plenty of buttery breadcrumbs. Then I take a pre-heated cast-iron pan, put in the crubeen skin-side down, and pop it in the oven to cook at about 220°C for somewhere between ten and twenty minutes. The toping should be golden brown, and the skin should have crisped up. I like to have that with a simple green salad.

There are all sorts of other things you can do with a crubeen, of course. The great chef Pierre Koffmann famously stuffed his with black pudding, and a lot of restaurants serve dainty little cross-sections of crubeen with all sorts of mousse-lines and the like in the middle. In fact, the first time I ever ate a crubeen was at Restaurant Patrick Guilbaud, and it certainly didn't look like a pig's foot.

An Australian chef, Paul Merrony (of London's Giaconda Dining Room), simply takes out the bones, chops up what's left, and forms it into little patties. He then fries them on a hot pan until a crust forms. These he serves with egg mayonnaise – an unexpected but lovely combination.

I have heard reports of people deep-frying pieces of cooked crubeen. I reckon this would need to be done very carefully, though, as the skin has a tendency to 'spit' when it gets really hot. But I do like the theory.

You see, the ideal crubeen for me has a crispy exterior and a melthing, almost liquid centre. Chefs like Fred Cordonnier of The Brown Bear in County Kildare spend a great deal of time turning them into little croquettes or *beignets* in order to get this effect. Which, to be honest, is more than I'm prepared to do for myself.

It's time we rediscovered the crubeen. If you like it simply boiled and dished up in the wake of what is usually referred to as a 'rake of pints', that's fine by me. I think most of us, however, would be more likely to take to the deconstructed-and-then-reconstructed crubeen. Either way, they are cheap, nutritious, and very tasty indeed. And if you eat enough of them, the natural gelatine will make your hair shine. What's not to like?

My crubeen crusade starts here and now. I will be sniffing out restaurants who have a way with the piggy's foot, and I'll be tracking down recipes, both ancient and modern. And most of all, I'll be encouraging people to rediscover a taste and a texture that would have been very familiar in Ireland a century ago, when waste was still a sin.

Drisheen

Some of the most wonderful dishes of the world are, by origin, the food of the poor. You only have to think of Tuscan bread salads and the French 'poor man's asparagus', to say nothing of all those slow-cooked cheap cuts, to realise this.

But I don't get drisheen. It didn't originate as the food of the poor, because Cork, where it was first dreamed up, was a very prosperous port, which, from the early eighteenth century, grew rich by provisioning the Royal Navy. Vast amounts of butter and beef and bacon went through the port of Cork.

Drisheen was originally made from sheep's blood and is flavoured with tansy, a pretty but very bitter-tasting wild herb. I find its jelly-like consistency and flavour, which is best described as essence of offal, absolutely revolting. Often served with tripe – especially in Limerick, where the local version is known as 'packet' – it is a traditional dish that I never want to taste again.

TV dinners

When I was at an impressionable age, somewhere around twelve, I was a keen viewer of a TV programme called *The Galloping Gourmet*. It was very much of its time, i.e. the early 1970s, as can be seen from the use of the word 'gourmet' without any obvious sense of irony. And the fact that the personable Australian presenter, Graham Kerr, regularly swigged his way through a bottle of wine in the course of each episode.

These days, the forces of political correctness would have him slaking his thirst with Evian. Maybe even green tea.

Somewhat before my time came the formidable Fanny Craddock, wearing a fresco of make-up and the kind of clothes that would make Barbara Cartland seem like Coco Chanel, and bearing a toxic grudge against her long-suffering and rather hopeless husband Johnny, who appeared on set solely as a target for her ire.

It's bizarre to think that the Craddocks were amongst the hottest properties in television in the 1960s, bigger than Gordon and Jamie and Nigella combined – for the simple reason that there was no competition.

A lot of people believe that we here in Ireland had no celebrity cooks; that this was the preserve of the BBC. But nothing could be further from the truth. I can just about remember Jimmy Flahive, who was chef at Dublin Airport at a time when it was, by the standards of the day, a breathtakingly sophisticated place to eat, appearing on dozens of black-and-white *Late Late Show*s. His best trick was slicing onions – very finely, at Formula One speed, and without drawing a drop of blood. All of Ireland would collectively hold its breath as Jimmy wielded the Sabatier.

Maura Laverty was, as they say, huge in the 1950s and 1960s. A creative writer by instinct, she larded her cookbooks with homely little stories of how good food and true love come together, even for the most confirmed of bachelors and spinsters in the bleakest bits of old Ireland. Her monumental book *Full and Plenty*, published by the Irish Flour Millers in 1960, was the cookbook with which I grew up. I still have my late mother's copy and return to it time and time again. The food is plain but wholesome, light on the garlic and the red wine, but sound, solid and built on the best of foundations.

In 1963, the Irish television audience, still dazzled by the new technology, were treated to a live cookery show presented by Monica Sheridan. *Monica's Kitchen* was a milestone in Irish television but also, according to those who can remember, a milestone in Irish food.

This sharp-featured, middle-aged woman, a Killiney housewife married to a barrister, was an instant hit. Her natural spontaneous wit and occasionally outrageous comments meant that viewers hung on her every word. And just as Nigella licks her fingers, so too did Monica Sheridan. But not in quite the same way. The finger-licking caused a good deal of outrage, and there were unconfirmed reports that shocked domestic-science teachers were considering presenting a mass petition to RTÉ.

Perhaps Monica Sheridan licked her fingers once too often on Teilifís Éireann. But she certainly galvanised the viewers, and she won a coveted Jacob's Award for her series in 1963. Whether it was too hot for RTÉ, I can't establish at this stage, but *Monica's Kitchen* did not go into a second series.

However, she published a book to accompany her TV debut: *Monica's Kitchen*, brought out by Castle Publications in 1963, is one of my most treasured possessions. It still crops up second-hand very frequently – a testament to how many copies were originally sold.

Opening it at random, I read: 'When I was a girl learning school-French, I thought that *oeufs à la coq* were special eggs laid by perverted French roosters. It was a great disappointment to discover that they were just ordinary boiled eggs. *Oeufs cocotte* didn't sound very respectable either but they are, alas, nothing you couldn't write home about.'

She is fascinating about garlic. 'Thirty years ago [i.e. in the 1930s], garlic was in daily use in kitchens all over Ireland. . . . In our house in the country, they put it into the food – and into the whiskey. Toothache, tonsils, stomachache, and all other internal complaints were doctored with the same medicine – two or three cloves of garlic crushed, and wet with half a glass of whiskey. This was poured down the patient's throat without a by-your-leave. It was a nauseating brew, enough to put anyone off whiskey for life.' But not garlic. She goes on: 'To me, the smell of raw garlic is the nicest of all, but, if you come into your house on a cold evening, and smell a stew that has a few cloves of garlic in it, it will remind you of the little bistros in Paris, and Gauloise cigarettes, and strolling down the Champs Élysées.'

Despite her affluent life in Killiney with maid and au pair (with whom she once cooked some garden snails, the subject of her funniest writing), Monica Sheridan had grown up as one of fourteen children on a farm in rural Ireland. She loved classic cooking but never lost her down-to- earth common sense. It was something she valued.

'There's nothing to cooking except ordinary common sense,' she says in *Monica's Kitchen*. 'You need a keen nose to smell burning, strong hands that can stand heat, and an occasional sense of wild extravagance coupled with a passion for economy. . . . Cooking has little to do with recipes, which are dead things and all read like a doctor's prescription. Unless you are a complete dud, you need never worry about them. But if you've a real interest in food, a love of experiment, and the courage to try anything once – you can forget about caution and calories.'

There was a delightful lack of reverence about Monica Sheridan, best exemplified by some of her comments on beef. 'Passing through a fair,' she says, 'in, say, Mullingar, you will see four-year-old Irish bullocks in the very pink of condition. They have the roving eyes and debonair looks of first-year medical students. A little gauche, perhaps, but nonetheless proud sons of bovine fathers. Give them a few more years and they could become a danger to the parish; but now is the time to kill them and eat them, when they are in their youthful prime.' It's hard to imagine Nigella Lawson or even Hugh Fearnley-Whittingstall writing in these terms.

And her honesty is peculiarly endearing. 'I once made ravioli,' she wrote. 'But the whole operation was so painful and so tedious that I cannot even bring myself to write about it.' I can't help wishing that she had managed to record the disaster.

Not a single second of Monica Sheridan on Teleifís Éireann survives. And I can't find anyone who remembers her television series in any detail. (I wish I had a euro for everyone who merely said: 'Oh yes, the woman who licked her fingers . . . .') She went on to write a book on Irish food for the American market (*My Irish Cookbook*) in 1965; she died in 1998.

She was a true original. True to her agricultural upbringing, to the traditional cooking skills she learned from her great-grandmother (who had lived through the Famine) and true to the essence of good food. Equally at home with a *coq au vin* or corned beef and cabbage, she might have done a great deal of good if her television career had not been cut short – not least in persuading us of how good Irish food can be.

Finger-lickin' good.

Bolognese sauce

I can't quite remember when spaghetti Bolognese came to our house, but I'd guess it was about 1972. The exotic aspect of it was not so much the sauce (although the fact that it contained garlic was a matter of pride) but the matter of eating pasta.

Indeed, it wasn't so much the pasta – my sister had introduced us to macaroni cheese a short time earlier – but the fact that it involved eating *spaghetti*. Spaghetti was seen only in films. Or cartoons. And if you remember the pasta scene in *Lady and the Tramp*, you may well imagine how we formed the view that the eating of spaghetti involved skill, and certain risks.

Bolognese was, if you like, a great move forward. It involved tomato puree from tubes – something I had never seen before – small quantities of garlic (again, something I had heard about but was now seeing for the first time) and, odd as it may seem, a pinch of Goodall's mixed herbs. Which, by the way, I don't advise – even if it was the closest thing to oregano that my mother could lay hands on. Oregano is for *pizzaiola* sauce, not for a ragu – which is what you toss into your spaghetti to make it in the true Bolognese manner.

In my university days, we all cooked a form of spaghetti Bolognese, for the simple reason that it involved mince and could be made on two gas rings. The more daring amongst us used extra garlic in a daredevil kind of way (we are talking 1980 here), and I added the mixed herbs. It was ghastly stuff, but we were hungry. We have to remember that the speciality of one of my contemporaries, who was not quite up to making Bolognese, was Knorr minestrone soup with plenty of curry powder added. It's hard to credit now, but I ate it with relish.

The great problem with Bolognese sauce is that, in theory, it's too easy. G. K. Chesterton once said that if a thing is worth doing, it's worth doing badly, and while I would tend to agree in general, I have to say that the world would be a better place if Bolognese sauce was never attempted by those who are not interested in making a good fist of it. You have to accept that this is not a quick dish. Indeed, the slower the cooking, the better.

You see, Bolognese sauce is not minced beef cooked with tomatoes, onions, garlic and a stock cube. And yet, every night of the week, this convenient concoction is produced in, oh . . . three out of every ten Irish households.

Proper Bolognese is another matter altogether. There is no single recipe, but some principles should always apply. The minced beef should be properly aged and suitably lean. Minced shin beef, if you can get it, is the way to go. You can add pancetta or bacon, or even a chicken liver, but that's up to you. However, you need to produce a very fine dice of carrot, onion, garlic and celery – each fragment no larger than a grain of rice – and soften it in a mixture of butter and decent olive oil. Then add the mince and cook it through while stirring, before adding plenty of dry white wine. Let this evaporate before adding good tinned chopped tomatoes (not the rank-smelling cheap ones) and some meat stock, ideally made from a good chicken carcass. As this reduces, add a bay leaf, lots of black pepper and some salt. When the mixture has become fairly dry, add some more stock and a dash of milk or cream. Then put it in a casserole and pop it into a very cool oven (e.g. the bottom oven of an Aga) for three hours, or even more. Believe me, you'll taste the difference.

I don't know where my mother got the recipe for her pioneering sauce, which was certainly the first Bolognese cooked on Grace Park Road, and possibly even in Drumcondra. But I do know that when I went on a school trip to Rome in 1975 we ate something very similar, with penne, and got to drink Frascati. And whatever about the effects of the wine, I discovered that penne is a lot easier to eat than spaghetti when you're a novice.

Rissoles

Rissoles. What a dread word. It means leftover meat minced up, formed into patties and fried until dry and tasteless. Rissoles were the staple diet of many households on Mondays. And in the unluckiest ones, even Tuesdays.

We rarely had anything left over from the Sunday roast. And when we did, it went into sandwiches or, bizarrely, got sliced, dipped in batter and fried by my mother, who had a healthy disregard for healthy eating.

No, what we called rissoles in our house were made from minced beef mixed with finely chopped onion, salt, pepper and a good dash of Worcestershire sauce. This mixture was formed into patties and fried on the pan until the outside was brown and a little bit crusty, while the interior was moist and fragrant with the onion and the Lea & Perrins.

Yes, I know what you're thinking. These were hamburgers in all but name. But I don't think of them that way – possibly because they were resolutely called rissoles. And because they would be eaten with creamy mashed potato and peas. No, no, hamburgers are a different class of thing altogether.

Fungophilia

When I was a teenager, I found that Sundays at home tended to drag. I preferred being out. Indeed, I preferred being out under the sky, and I didn't mind much if I got soaked to the skin or caught a dose of exposure on the hillsides of Wicklow. Anything was better than the tedium of being at home.

I also liked the idea of going out and making the wild harvest, gathering in the bounty of hedgerows by way of the Number 84 bus. And I was madly in love with Felicity Kendall from *The Good Life*, which made it all seem so worthwhile.

Oh yes, there were blackberries, which went into jam. And rowan berries from the mountain ash trees, which made quite a good jelly. But best of all were the wild mushrooms.

And they still are. Lots of them. This is because the average Irish person would rather bathe in the outflow from Sellafield than eat a feral fungus – a mushroom from anywhere other than the supermarket.

It would be very different if we adopted the Italian approach. The *carabinieri* in rural areas are trained to identify edible fungi, so you can have your basketful checked out by the local police. (For some reason, this conjures up a picture of a Garda asking: 'Are you de owner of dis toadstool?') Alternatively, you can have the job done by the village pharmacist, who is legally obliged to provide the service.

Of course, even with these safeguards, Italy records

several mushroom-related deaths every year. I suppose where fungus foraging is commonplace, people can become careless or over-adventurous. Or maybe they were just a bit unhinged in the first place.

The Russians and the eastern Europeans are even greater fungophiles than the Italians and French. Indeed, many Poles insist on eating a particular mushroom which has such a high heavy-metal content that it's shunned in the rest of Europe. More than ten years ago, I stumbled across what appeared to be the entire staff of the Russian embassy combing some woodland in Wicklow for ceps.

My first mushroom foray, as a teenager, involved shameless trespassing in the woods of the Kilruderry estate near Bray. I headed off with my guidebook, mildly excited by the whiff of danger, and enchanted by the autumn colours. I returned with masses of edible fungi, and I've never looked back. In the autumn, I can't pass a patch of woodland without experiencing a strong urge to get down on my hands and knees and search for what the books call, in their quaint way, 'choice edibles'. In fact, if the weather is any way good (which is seldom), I regard time spent not looking for, or eating, wild mushrooms as being more or less wasted. The season is short: I don't want to waste any time.

But what's the appeal of wild mushrooms? Well, it's wild food, as organic as it gets. It's free – if you write off the hours spent scrambling over an inhospitable landscape and getting scratched and stung. The pursuit offers some fairly healthy exercise (and the risk of a broken limb, which only adds to the excitement). But most of all, wild mushrooms taste wonderful.

If you bring your pan to the woods and cook them *sur place*, as the French would say, so much the better. Just as there is no sausage that tastes as good as the charred one that has been rather insensitively cooked on a stick at the camp fire, no mushrooms ever smell, let alone taste, as good as the ones you cook in the open air.

The big, fat, white field mushroom (Agaricus campestris), with pink or brown gills, is the definitive wild mushroom. It's closely related to the ones you buy in the supermarket – in every way but its flavour, which is superb.

Field mushrooms are becoming very rare because they hate the high levels of artificial nitrogen to which Irish grasslands are routinely subjected. You need old pasture with low levels of fertility, and there's not much of that left. Our paddock started to produce mushrooms only four years after we acquired it and stopped using fertiliser on it.

If you want to go searching for wild mushrooms to eat, let me give you some encouragement – and a word or two of caution. It's fun, but not risk-free. Although there are relatively few mushrooms which are lethal, quite a lot of them can make you very sick. The really deadly ones, however, look very innocent and work in very unpleasant ways.

The very ordinary-looking Death Cap, *Amanita phalloides*, is particularly cruel. After an initial bout of sickness, the patient will appear to recover, only to suffer fatal liver and kidney failure. Its close relative, the Destroying Angel, *Amanita virosa*, is very nearly as poisonous. Sorry about the Latin names but, let's face it, it's important that we know what we're talking about.

The key thing is to arm yourself with a really good guide to wild mushrooms, one that has excellent illustrations.

Never pick any mushroom that you cannot positively identify, right down to the finest detail. And remember that you need specimens at all stages of development in order to make an identification.

The best approach is to find an expert who is prepared to take you under their wing. And if you have the slightest doubt about what something is, don't eat it. I reckon I know the difference between the deadly poisonous *Amanita pantherina* and its near-doppelgänger, the delicious *Amanita rubescens*, but I just wouldn't risk it.

The good old field mushroom is fairly easy to identify, but beware of its lookalike, the Yellow Stainer. The flesh of the Yellow Stainer bruises yellow; while it won't kill you, it could make you very unwell.

Parasol mushrooms (*Lepiota procera*) are very distinctive, and only the very small members of this family are poisonous. This was the first wild mushroom that I picked and ate, and the easiest to identify.

Ceps (*Boletus edulis*) are the most delicious members of the *Boletus* family. They are unusual in having a sponge-like texture where other mushrooms have gills. Most *Boletus* are edible, and none that grow in Ireland are deadly.

Chanterelles, which are sometimes called 'girolles', are probably my favourite. There are two kinds: the slightly dowdy-looking *Cantharellus tubaeformis* and the bright, apricot-coloured *Cantharellus cibarius*. Both are very hard to mistake for anything else if you follow your guidebook to the letter, and both are very good to eat. The *cibarius* is better – fleshier and stronger – and, with its bright orange/yellow colouring, easy enough to spot amongst the beech leaves.

With chanterelles, I like to fry them in butter and then mix them with some cream, a couple of beaten eggs, a little salt and black pepper and some freshly grated nutmeg. Then I put this mixture in a pastry case and bake until I have a delicious, wild mushroom tart. For me, this is one of the greatest delicacies. I eat it with a glass of white wine and a glow of satisfaction when I think about how much chanterelles imported from France cost here. Talk about local food.

You can keep your foie gras and your caviar. Give me the free stuff from the woods any day.

Vegetarians

A lot of vegetarians don't look terribly healthy. If you're going to exclude meat from your diet, you need to be aware of other sources of iron. And as Dr John Briffa keeps pointing out, there is nothing at all healthy about eating masses and masses of carbohydrates, which seems to be what most vegetarians do. Vegetarianism is not, by definition, a healthier diet than that enjoyed by omnivores. Which, by the way, is what I am. Just because I eat meat doesn't make me a carnivore – while being a vegetarian certainly makes some people unbearably self-righteous.

It's not easy being a vegetarian, and if you don't like pulses, it might be wisest not to try it. People become vegetarian for all sorts of reasons. To take just two famous vegetarians, I wonder if Adolf Hitler and George Bernard Shaw shared similar motivations. And I apologise for mentioning the latter: vegetarians must be sick and tired of being reminded by cheery omnivores of this rather irritating factoid.

The restaurant writer A. A. Gill has said that vegetarians are people who take pleasure in not eating things. Which is a very good line. But I don't think it's always true. A lot of vegetarians, it strikes me, are just not very interested in food. Pleasure, beyond assuaging mere hunger, doesn't really enter into it. There can be a puritan streak in vegetariansim that puts a real damper on the sheer sensuous joy of eating well.

Denis Cotter's Café Paradiso in Cork produces some of the greatest meat-free dishes that you will ever encounter, but the average vegetarian meal is so heavy on dietary fibre that the bowels start heaving just at the sight of it. And why is there always so much? Is it some kind of compensation?

Some vegetarians are motivated by the simple fact that there is something obscene in converting vast quantities of grain into meat when millions of people are starving and could use that grain just as grain. Some believe that it is cruel and wasteful to rear and then kill animals for food. Others are horrified at the notion of eating organisms which are much closer to us in evolutionary terms than vegetables and pulses. Pigs, for example, are as intelligent as dogs, if not more so, and their internal organs are very similar to our own (though no less delicious for that).

No matter which of these broad categories of vegetarianism one might belong to, there is something hypocritical about eating eggs and dairy produce which have been produced according to the principles of factory farming. Most well-informed people are aware of the cruelty involved in battery-egg production. It is, quite simply, indefensible.

Milk production is another matter. How many consumers of milk and cheese have witnessed the mourning of cows for lost calves? Perhaps it's something we should think about. On the other hand, cattle have been bred for hundreds of years with dairying in mind. There is no going back, I suppose. You certainly can't release cattle into the wild, as some of the loonier animal-rights activists would have us do.

Vegans eat only produce of plant origin and, as a result, are advised to take dietary supplements to compensate for what they are missing. The fact is, we have evolved in such a way that we require a diet involving eggs and milk if we eschew meat completely. There's no easy answer; food is complicated.

There's no doubt that we eat far too much meat, and that the vast bulk of that meat comes from factory farming. Some religions, notably Judaism, have strict dietary laws which date from the pre-scientific age. Jewish orthodoxy embraces all manner of technological advances, including GM, while not obviously caring for the welfare of animals or the planet in general. The laws date not just from the pre-scientific age but from a time when nobody got sentimental about animals.

But wouldn't it be great to think that a major world religion might introduce dietary guidelines which would aim to support sustainable agriculture and good health? I don't think we should hold our collective breath. Many people adopt such practices on the basis of their own, individual spirituality.

And it is a spiritual question. Judaism was originally deeply concerned with the issue of clean food and general hygiene. As a result, fewer Jews died during the Black Death, and this gave the slapdash Christians the opportunity to accuse their 'separated brethren' of poisoning the wells. It was only a short jump from that to persecution.

But what can you eat with a clear conscience these days? Vegetables, certainly, if they have been grown with minimal inputs. Meat, in small quantities, provided it has not been intensively reared. Fish, but only the few that are not endangered.

Yes, there's nothing simple about eating ethically, but maybe being vegetarian makes it slightly easier.

Auntie May

My great-aunt, May Murray, spent World War Two running the Arundell Arms on the River Tamar in Devon. It has always been one of the great fishing hotels of England, and Auntie May brought the same standards home to her 'private hotel', as she called it, just off Fitzwilliam Square.

Actually, it was what most of us would call a guest house. She ran this establishment, divided over five Georgian floors, from her bed, and depended on the elderly Frances, a dour housekeeper from Wexford, and William, 'my butler', as she referred to him. William was usually attired in a white mess jacket and was frequently the worse for wear, being exceptionally keen on the Crested Ten.

I used to visit Auntie May once a week, after school, usually on Wednesday afternoons. I associate her particularly with a peculiarly Irish sweet, the iced caramel. This was, and still is, a shockingly sugary confection, being, essentially, a combination of butter and sugar in the form of chewy toffee, encased in a crisp coating of, er . . . sugar. They still come, as they always did, in two kinds: pink and white. And if you can discern any difference in taste between them, you're a better man than I am, Gunga Din. In those far-off days, iced caramels were made by a company called Clarnico, and they came in boxes. Nowadays, they seem to be softer in the centre than before, and they come in bags.

Auntie May was also keen on violet creams. These were small chocolates containing a fondant which was both flavoured with and coloured violet. On top of the dark-chocolate shell was a single crystallised violet petal. The taste was, well, very strongly violety, and the sweetness of the fondant was only just cut by the darkness of the chocolate.

I have an idea that Auntie May's violet creams came from Fuller's, which was a shop and café in Grafton Street in those days. I have since rediscovered them in Charbonnel et Walker's in London, where they go one further and sell pink rose creams. They are very good indeed in a decadent kind of way, but nothing comes close to the haunting, ethereal fragrance of violet creams.

My great-aunt's palate was probably pretty blunted by constant exposure to untipped cigarettes. Her room was littered with empty red Benson & Hedges tins, the occasional pack of Senior Service, and Churchman's No. 1. So it's probably not surprising that her favourite restorative was sweet, red Cinzano, a bottle of which she used to keep close to the radiator – which pumped out heat all year round. She would occasionally offer me a taste of this vile and tepid liquid, and I occasionally felt it only polite to accept. It nearly put me off drink for life.

Auntie May would frequently bring me across the road to the Grey Door, one of the few 'proper' restaurants that Dublin had left since the closure of Jammet's. At least, that's what she told me. It was my first experience of dining out, and I thought it was terribly grand.

More often, she would order dinner at home. A bottle of wine would be produced, always rather dusty and venerable, hauled up from the cellar by the often-unsteady William. By the time I was twelve, I would be allowed a small glass, and I know now that it must have been good stuff.

The wine, I later discovered, was a legacy from some strange Belgian, allegedy a viscount, with whom Auntie May had been on imtimate terms during the war. He disappeared one day, leaving her a lot of claret. This meant that I got to drink pre-war claret on a regular basis during my formative years. I have to say that when I first tasted great old Bordeaux as a grown-up, it seemed spookily familiar.

The wine I took for granted – and I wasn't terribly keen on it in those days. No, what I really enjoyed about these *dîners à deux* with my great-aunt was the fact that dessert was invariably Epicure tinned cherries with pouring cream. This, for a long time in my young life, was my idea of heaven. But I would have found it just as hard to persuade my parents of it as to get them to start buying pre-war claret.

The Aga

Only one cooker has so far given its name to a genre of literary fiction. The Aga Saga, as written by the likes of Mary Wesley and Joanna Trollope, tends to be a cosy read with a country theme.

A Rayburn Saga doesn't have the same ring, although these ranges are made by the same company. Agas are dearer and, in an aspirational world, perhaps more desirable. But they are much more just a status symbol, redolent of country houses, green gumboots and well-thumbed copies of *Horse and Hound*.

But what exactly is an Aga? It was invented, in very much the same form as exists today, by Gutav Dahlen, a Danish scientist, in the early 1920s. Essentially, it's a cast-iron range that holds a vast reservoir of heat. The heat source was traditionally solid fuel, such as coke, and the daily stoking and raking was quite a chore. These days, Agas are fuelled by oil, gas and even electricity.

The four-oven Aga is a vast affair, well suited to the feeding of a small army – or institution. We make do very happily with the two-oven version. On top there are two plates, each thoroughly insulated by heavy hinged lids. When you want to use these, for simmering or boiling respectively, you pull up the lid and cook. Below, there's a roasting oven and a simmering or warming oven, in which you can slow-cook for hours without fear of burning, or produce amazingly intense semi-dried tomatoes.

It's interesting to think that while brick ovens are becoming very fashionable these days, Agas essentially do the same job, and rather more conveniently. That is, they provide a great deal of dry heat, using iron rather than brick.

On a practical level, an Aga is the best source of heat for drying clothes and swimming gear and damp boots. It's not entirely true to say that it will do your ironing for you, but there's no doubt that if you fold the clothes, especially sheets, when they come off the clothes line, and plonk them on top of the Aga (with the lids closed!), they end up remarkably free of creases and, more importantly, smelling toastily and comfortingly of warm fabric.

Then, of course, there's Aga toast, made in a wire holder that fits between the hot plate and its hinged cover. There's no toast quite like it. It's like toast made in front of an open fire, but it's easier, and tastes even better.

Aga fanatics claim that their design classic will cook anything. This isn't true. The one thing the traditional Aga can't do is stir-frying. Agas are too gentle for that kind of thing.

But stuff will burn, all the same, and you won't smell it, because the ovens are vented so thoroughly. That's the only drawback as far as I'm concerned. But you get a lovely smell of cooking when you're out in the garden.

Aga owners tend to develop quite intimate relationships with their cookers. 'I never thought I could fall in love with a lump of metal, but I have', one of the smitten once said to me. Even in these days of universal central heating, they regard the Aga glow as an essential part of the kitchen. An Aga also seems to be the favourite kind of heat for animals. Just ask any Jack Russell terrier.

Enthusiasts invariably refer to their Agas as being the

heart of the household. They even forgive them for making the kitchen sweaty during the summer. Personally, I'd be inclined to turn it off.

In recent years, Aga have met the challenge of modern, instantly controllable cookers with innovations that combine the classic Aga look with gas hobs, electric fan ovens and all sorts of high-tech features. Traditionalists, of course, are inclined to scoff, but I have yet to meet one who wouldn't like to have an Aga Mini as an adjunct. The conventional Aga, however, far outsells all of Aga's new concessions to twenty-first-century life, not only here in Ireland but in the UK and North America too.

We tend to resist turning on the Aga again, after its summer holiday, until we can see our breaths condensing in the bracing autumn air. And that's in the kitchen. But in fact it's generally our children who demand the rekindling. It's not quite an ultimatum, but they make it pretty clear that we would all feel better if the kitchen had a bit of a glow and we didn't have to depend on a Baby Belling (splendid machine though it is in many ways) and a gas ring for cooking. And they are usually quite right. I still find myself putting a pot on the hotplate and trying to find the switch, but it's lovely to be able to cook without waiting for the oven to warm up. And it's bloody good to warm the posterior against the Aga's polished rail while we watch the rain obscure the otherwise rather lovely view.

This, it can be argued, is environmental vandalism. George Monbiot claimed, in 2009, that running an Aga (ours is oil-fired) is a pretty inexcusable thing to do. But he got his figures wrong, saying that a large coal-fired Aga produces nine times the CO_2 output of the average home, whereas, in fact, it produces 35 percent more. These figures were corrected in due course. The piece was headed: 'This is indeed a class war, and the campaign against the Aga starts here'.

Now, let's consider, for a moment, that we are talking about the large (four-oven) Aga as against the much more common two-oven version. And that most Agas run on either gas or oil. The Aga, large or small, reduces the call for central heating to a minimum, obviates the need for a separate cooker, produces as much hot water as anyone could want and renders the tumble-dryer pretty well redundant. At that rate of going, given that a big coal-fired Aga produces 35 percent more CO_2 than the average home, it's not unreasonable to suspect that the smaller Aga, run on gas or oil, might actually mean that the household around which it gathers produces less CO_2 than the average. Or at least the same. And, in terms of class war (something that seems to obsess the English, God bless them), I would stress that our Aga was second-hand and cost less than many of the electric cookers that adorn those trophy kitchens in which very little, if any, cooking is actually done.

Anyway, I'm not going to get hung up on figures. Life is short, and in our own case we grow much of what we eat and don't take long-haul flights very often (or even as often as we might like), and we recycle like mad, despite the difficulty of doing so in this little country of ours.

The day of the latest rekindling of the Aga was marked in a suitably autumnal way with organic chicken thighs and legs pot-roasted with freshly gathered chanterelles, butter, garlic and a bit of cream. We simply sweated down the mushrooms until all the inevitable moisture had evaporated and the flavour had intensified, then added a glass of white wine, the chicken and some seasoning. Then put the lot, covered, into the Aga for the better part of two hours and stirred in the cream at the end, giving it a bit of heat to thicken the sauce. And then a tarte tatin of windfall Cox's Orange Pippins and plump wild blackberries from just outside the door.

Anyway, it's odd to think that the Aga was originally a Danish invention, as it seems particularly suited to the Irish climate. Ideally, we would like to run ours on wood pellets or even our own biomass but, for the time being, we will continue to feed it oil. Our central heating has been turned on for a total of about seventy-two hours over the past three years. We have depended on the background heat of our gallant little Aga and our couple of wood-burning stoves (fuelled, in the main, from our own logs), reasonable insulation, and decent sweaters. Clothes are the unsung heroes of the fight against the cold and the damp, and they are pretty well unbeatable for sustainability.

The soft stuff

Yes, of course, there was Coke and Pepsi and 7-Up and Fanta. There was even an orange fizz called Mirinda (which still exists in many parts of the world, as PepsiCo's answer to Coca-Cola's Fanta). And I used to quench the after-school thirst on late-June afternoons with the stuff in a shop called Donnelly's on Philipsburgh Avenue, often snaffling a cream doughnut as well.

But these were the glamorous brands amongst the soft drinks. And I imagine that they were fairly recent arrivals, doing their damndest to oust the young nation's attachment to 'minerals' (often pronounced *minner-thals* in Dublin) – which, presumably, derived their collective name from the mineral waters which, long ago, were flavoured to produce a form of 'pop' or, as the Americans would say, soda.

Minerals were all Irish-made, and there was one amongst them which was unique to this island: red lemonade. One of the first things you learned, if you were staying in England during the holidays, was that British lemonade had no colour whatsoever. And this realisation educed a kind of pity. The first duty of lemonade, it seemed to us in those days, was to be red.

Actually, not so much red as a kind of rusty, tawny brown, but it was called red. The big brand was Taylor Keith, and its lemonade came in glass bottles with a rather sober (if you see what I mean) label. These days, it has become TK, it comes in huge plastic bottles, and the label looks like it was designed by Timothy Leary. TK is represented as a psychedelic explosion.

However, I suspect that the colour has changed somewhat. Maybe the original dyes are no longer approved for food use. There is certainly an urban myth that the reason red lemonade is available in Ireland is that we are the only country in the world *not* to have banned the colouring involved. This is complete nonsense, of course.

Nobody has yet written the history of red lemonade, and its origins are swathed in mystery. Nobody seems to be able to answer the question as to why lemonade became red in Ireland while remaining colourless in the rest of these islands. It does seem likely, though, that the drink emerged in the closing years of the nineteenth century. Every town of any standing in those days had its mineral-water factory – encouraged perhaps by Father Mathews' success with the Pledge. There was Stafford's in Wexford, Deasy's in Clonakilty, Nash's in County Limerick and Williams's in Tullamore, to name just a few of the bigger operators.

It does seem that Nash's, founded in 1875, were amongst the first, if not *the* first, to make red lemonade. The original recipe is a closely guarded secret to this day. And Deasy's, curiously, were making white lemonade from Victorian times, only launching the red version during World War Two.

I was rather surprised to see, in one of London's first upmarket burger restaurants, that 'Irish red lemonade' was being flagged as a bit of a delicacy. I'm not so sure. It's fine with Pimm's and a few sprigs from the herb garden, but I'm not sure I'd fancy it any other way.

Sparkling lemonade, of whatever colour, would not have been possible if the English scientist Joseph Priestley had not discovered how to carbonate water – or, as he put, how to 'impregnate water' with 'fixed air'. I remember big, heavy glass soda syphons at home. These were bought, with a deposit, and then returned for a refill. They had a spout and a little lever at the top for dispensing the fizzy water. In some homes – but not in our virtually teetotal one – the soda syphon and the whiskey bottle stood together on the sideboard. The names I can recall are Cantrell & Cochrane (which became better known as C&C, or Club) and Thwaite's. Soda syphons, which were rather impressive and elegant things, were on the way out by the time I was in short pants. It was becoming easier, and cheaper, simply to bottle fizzy water.

Barley water

I have never really 'got' sport – which must have been quite a disappointment to my father. Being the only son of someone who not only ran and played football for his school but *boxed* for it as well demanded some show of enthusiasm on my part. I managed a little.

My school was obsessed with rugby and, for a while, a little of this obsession rubbed off on me. But the only game I ever really enjoyed playing – I asked to go for lessons – was tennis. And this is why I came to think that Robinson's barley Water was a much more glamorous drink than it really is.

I used to watch Wimbledon solidly for the two weeks it was on every year. I hugely envied the ball boys, who were about my age, and their green and purple uniforms. And their easy access to all that Robinson's barley water.

Indeed, the Robinson's TV advertising positively dripped with Wimbledon imagery. And am I imagining it, or did they get the silky-voiced (and hugely irritating) Dan Maskell to do the voice-over? I seem to remember him as the elderly gent who was madly in love with Virginia Wade . . .

My mother occasionally made a far superior home-made version of this cloudy, lemon-flavoured drink (I believed that lemon was the only allowable flavour for the stuff) by boiling pearl barley in water until all the goodness had been extracted, then adding sugar, lemon juice and lemon rind. It was good stuff, but I still preferred the Robinson's concentrated product – which shows how branding can get to you.

They say it's nutritious: I suppose it must be better than your average fizzy drink, although the commercially available version is pretty high in sugar.

Barley water, like cranberry juice, is said to be good for cystitis. This is a rather less glamorous recommendation than its association with international tennis.

Bottled fruit

There were other bottled fruits of which we had heard, but the common-or-garden generic form of bottled fruit was bottled plums.

Anyone who grew up in the sixties with a well-stocked garden, especially one with a bit of room, will have been nurtured with the fruit of the remarkable plum variety called 'Victoria'. When it was introduced, in the declining years of Queen Victoria's reign, it was revolutionary. For a start, it was self-fertile (and didn't need another plum variety for cross-pollination), and the fruit were big, beautiful, full of flavour and, most significantly, amazingly bountiful.

The bottling of Victoria plums was a ceremony which marked the end of August, and for many will always be associated with the impending return to school.

There would be steaming cauldrons of glistening syrup and other steaming pans of water, in which the Kilner jars (remember them?) would stand, waiting to be sterilised. And above all, there was the distinctive smell of warm sugar and hot fruit.

The idea was clever: sugar is a preservative, Kilner jars are airtight, and the application of heat dispatched any rogue bacterium that happened to be lurking on either the plums or the glassware.

Bottled plums could be kept for years, laid down like fine wines. Given a little time, the colour would migrate from the mottled skins into the syrup, turning it a lovely, deep tawny red. Spooned over the fruit, and with some fresh cream swirled in, it was a luxury.

More commonly, bottled plums were seen as a little frugal – the kind of thing that was served to the family, as distinct from guests. And it tended to be served with custard rather than cream, for the same reason.

A few years ago, I saw that tradition being broken at a birthday dinner in a lovely old house in County Down. The forty or so guests finished with bottled plums from the walled garden, the syrup fortified with a good slug of brandy. Crumbled meringues and whipped cream turned this dish into a delight for the senses.

We have two Victoria plum trees at our home in Cork. They produce so much fruit that whole limbs fall off under the weight of the harvest. I can pick a couple of trugs of plums, and the trees still look much the same. We don't bottle them, of course, but it might be tempting to do so, for old times' sake. Instead, we simply split them, take the stones out, and freeze the fruit. Frozen plums make a fine crumble in deepest winter and, unlike the bottled kind, are not full of sugar.

I suppose you could argue that bottling is more 'sustainable' than freezing because it depends on sugar, heat and airlessness rather than the steady trickle of electricity that the freezer feeds on. And there's no doubt that an occasional sugar rush can be fun.

Yes, bottling plums. It's like travelling back in time.

Pear-fection

I suppose it ill behoves us to laugh at the more ludicrous aspects of the EU, given that there is such scope for hilarity back home with our own bureaucrats, let alone our democratically elected government.

After many years of, let's just call it weirdness, the EU decided to allow fruit and vegetables that are imperfectly shaped to be sold. They came, at last, to realise that nature does not deliver, on demand, fresh produce that conforms to any directives at all. And while I joined the farmers' organisations and the organic movement in welcoming this move, I only barely restrained myself from tearing out my greying hairs at the very thought that such a move took so long.

Anyone who has ever grown their own fruit and vegetables will know that they come in all shapes and sizes. And they will also know that flavour and nutrition – the reasons why we eat such produce – are no respecters of physical perfection.

In any case, physical perfection is rather suspect. It smacks of eugenics and fascism and a touch of the master race. Perfection, in any sphere, is pretty dull. In terms of physical attraction between human beings, it's the lack of perfect facial symmetry, the freckles, the lop-sided grin, the hint of earthiness about an individual that we find uniquely appealing. Perfection is scary, alien and alienating.

While we should, I suppose, be singing and dancing in the streets now that the EU will allow us to buy fruits and vegetables just as God intended them, I am still a little

hung up on the matter of what type of minds could have
dreamed up the now-defunct regulations in the first place.
As it happens, I don't believe that the motivation was sinis-
ter. I'm of the view that it reflects, as so much negative
human activity does, a lack of enough things about which
to worry. Anxiety about nonsense, and the resulting impetus to boss people around, is born of a fearful combination
– a combination of an abundance of power and a complete
lack of understanding of the common good. Thus, a vacuum is created and utter tosh rushes in to fill it.

Did the Eurocrats genuinely believe that they were helping us consumers, or the farmers, or even the retailers,
when they decreed that, for example, aubergines had to
conform to a certain size, shape and weight? If they did –
and let's give them the benefit of the doubt for a moment
– they were surely seriously misguided.

No, I think they found time hanging heavy on their
hands, and felt they needed to exercise their power. By
telling us what kind of fresh produce we could buy, they
were validating, in a very perverse way, their function.

However, that's enough carping. Let us rejoice, as I say,
at a rare outbreak of sanity in the realms of Eurocracy. And
let us, too, consider what has happened. Before we run
away with ourselves.

There has been no change to the rules concerning the
top ten sellers, which include apples, tomatoes and strawberries. If such produce does not conform to the EU
Grade 1 and Grade 2 rules, it can still be sold (let joy be
unconfined!), but it will have to be marked 'for cooking'.

I think we should be the judge of that. On one occasion, I picked two kilos of strawberries from the garden.

The scent was fabulous, the shapes were various, the sizes likewise. We decided to freeze most of the crop for making into jam (strawberry jam is best made in small batches, otherwise the colour fades) and to eat the choicest and least slug-afflicted fruits with a little cream. To be honest, I didn't need the EU, or anyone else, to advise me on this. 'For cooking'? Forsooth!

I grow four or five varieties of tomato. One of them is commercially produced for processing into tomato paste and sauce bases and, to be fair, the fruits are fairly uniform. The rest are a commercial grower's nightmare. They come in all sizes, and they have thin skins that negate any hopes of a decent shelf-life. What they *do* have, however, is fantastic flavour.

And the curious thing is that one of them, the tomato Harbinger, was *the* commercial tomato variety in the years immediately after World War Two, when flavour was paramount. These days, you can sell tomatoes with all the taste of cotton wool, provided they look right.

So, while the EU is content to lay down the law, literally, about what size and shape of apple or strawberry we are allowed to buy for actual eating, they have no interest whatsover in flavour or quality. It's pretty emblematic of the world in which we now live. Style is everything, substance a mere detail.

Outside the big sellers, we are to be permitted to buy a whole range of fruit and vegetables in any size or shape that nature finds it in her bounty to deliver. I am beside myself with joy at the fact that any kind of apricots, artichokes, asparagus, aubergines, avocados, beans, Brussels sprouts, carrots, cauliflowers, cherries, courgettes, cucumbers, mushrooms, garlic, hazelnuts, cabbages, leeks, melons, onions, peas, plums, celery, spinach, walnuts, watermelons and chicory are just fine as far as EU bureaucrats are concerned.

Again, it matters not a jot what they taste like, but thank heaven for small mercies. Because if you find apricots or courgettes or chicory that are all different sizes, and possibly misshapen too, there's a fair chance that they will taste excellent. Nature will have seen to that, just as nature will have refused to recognise human-made rules and regulations. Good old nature, is my view.

Such is the nature of EU regulations that I was quite confused about the pivotal ruling on the, er . . . crucial banana issue. I had run away with the notion that the EU had given up on the mammoth task of straightening bananas (a rather presumptuous business, as the EU is hardly one of the world's great banana producers).

Just so that we can sleep easy in our beds, let us remind ourselves that, as far as the humble banana is concerned, the EU still decrees, and I quote: 'the thickness of a transverse section of the fruit between the lateral faces and the middle, perpendicular to the longitudinal axis, must be at a minimum 27mm'. I don't know about you, but when I go out to buy bananas, it's those 27 millimetres that outweigh all other considerations, such as ripeness, size, weight and flavour.

Banana standards are enshrined in EU Regulation 2257/94 of 16 September 1994. I just hope that they managed to do something worthwhile on that day, way back in 1994. But don't depend on it.

Back in the days when only Italians got to be pope, an

elderly Jesuit once explained to me how the papal teaching worked. 'The Italians know not to take all the rules seriously,' he said. 'It's only in Ireland and Poland that we do that.'

It's the same with Europe. We take the EU's more arcane rulings *very* seriously. We fail to realise that the French and the Spanish and the Italians have a much more à la carte approach to these things. Just visit a Continental market, and you will see that the stallholders pay not a blind bit of notice to such nonsense. They just carry on as they always have.

Apples

Those Dublin houses, the semi-detached three- and four-bedroomed houses that created the suburbs in the years just after World War Two, from Raheny to Mount Merrion, Ballymun to Kilmacud, very often seem to have come ready-equipped with a couple of apple trees.

In the late 1940s, there must have been a boom in sales of two of the most famous apple-tree varieties: Cox's Orange Pippin and the big, sour, greasy-skinned Bramley's Seedling. The latter is our favourite – almost our sole – cooking apple in Ireland, its tart flesh sweetened with plenty of sugar and encased in puff pastry. The former is one of the best eating apples. Perhaps *the* best.

Consider what Edward Bunyard had to say in *The Anatomy of Dessert*, published in 1929. (Despite its title, the book is a lyrical account of the pleasure of fruit.) 'November, then, for apple lovers, is the Cox's month, and this fruit needs no introduction or eulogy, the Château d'Yquem of apples and, to my taste, to be similarly used.' Well, times have changed, of course, and Château d'Yquem is used mainly by billionaires these days. By contrast, Cox's Orange Pippin, even when it is so good that it rivals this greatest of all dessert wines, is almost free.

Anyone who scrumped orchards will remember how the fruit was never ripe and how green apples gave us tummy trouble. Beneath our scruffy and often somewhat malodorous exterior, there lurked a tender little digestive tract which, while it was used to more conventional abuse, simply couldn't hack this kind of thing.

Apples are generally picked too early, as soon as they reach what we imagine to be the right size. Cox's, for example, will start to look really good towards the end of September but, as Mr Bunyan points out, they come into their own in November. The trick is to pick them in mid-October, or as soon as the skin is a lovely mixture or gold and dark red. Eat them then, by all means, but keep a few, wrapped in newspaper and stored in a cool place, until the next month, when they will be at their peak in terms of taste.

The other trick with Cox's, if you have an old tree that produces lots of fruit, is to thin the little apples in July so that the remaining ones have both the space and the resources to grow to a reasonable size. Cox's are never a big apple, but there's no reason why they should be as small as they usually are in the average garden.

It only occurs to me now that what we used to call 'apple tart' wasn't apple tart at all. A tart is an open affair: a pie with no top. My mother's 'apple tarts' were shallow pies, with the sliced Bramley fruit entirely enclosed in rough-puff pastry encrusted with sugar crystals, and apple-y syrup oozing through the vent holes.

That, for me, is the smell of childhood weekends: the scent of warm apple with cloves and the fragrance of hot flour and sugar hovering in the kitchen air.

Table manners

A few years ago, a schoolboy somewhere in the west of Ireland was sent home because his hair was deemed to be too long. 'Do you want people to think you're a girl?,' demanded his deeply sensitive (female) principal. It caused quite a fuss, and underlined for me how concerned we tend to be with appearances rather than substance.

I'm always amused at the presumption of the sort of restaurant that demands that male guests wear a jacket and tie. When translated into English, this means: 'Before we are prepared to relieve you of your money, we want you to dress according to our rules.' This makes no sense to me at all. It should be the customers who tell the restaurateurs how to dress.

Mind you, if I ran a restaurant I would probably impose a few rules. Mobile phones would be allowed, but only on the understanding that diners wishing to converse on them should step outside. Men wearing coloured shirts with white collars would not be admitted, on the simple basis that conspicuous displays of naffness interfere with the digestion. Surely that's reasonable?

I would also insist that diners be familar with the correct use of a knife and fork. Now, this may seem unusual. Surely most of us know how to wield these devices? Have a look around the next time you're eating out, and you will see people holding their knife like a pencil, or dispensing with it altogether and using the fork as a shovel. A remarkable number of people don't bother placing their knife and fork together when they've finished eating. I can only assume that they were never taught to do so.

Oddly enough, these are often the same people who are too dainty to pull a bread roll apart with their bare hands, and instead prod it with their butter knife. Children should be taught from the time they are in the high chair that bread rolls are for manual dismemberment. They enjoy the process.

We all need to be taught that while toothpicks are sometimes provided in restaurants (although I can't remember the last time I saw one), this does not mean that they should be used in public. If you need to use one, take it to the loo or the car park. And while we're at it, don't pick your nose or your ears either.

Knives and forks should not be used to add emphasis to what you are saying, and knives should not be held as if they are instruments for writing. This is a very common mistake but it still looks terrible. Napkins should not appear above the table during the meal, and they should never, ever, be tucked into the shirt. Unless you are under the age of four.

We were all warned about talking with your mouth full as children, and rightly too. I was once absent-mindedly told: 'Don't talk with you mouth open.'

But speaking through food is a hideous crime against society; partially masticated food is never a pretty sight, and there is always the danger that particles will fly out and assault a neighbour. People have sued for less.

Mind you, I've noticed that people tend to forget this as they get older and, having issued dire threats to their children about keeping their mouths firmly shut when eating, unconsciously display the contents of their gobs to all and sundry when they reach their riper years.

The decline and fall of the family dinner has not helped. Most people eat in front of the television these days, so it's not surprising that, when forced to sit at a restaurant table, they don't know what to do with their elbows, let alone the implements they are supposed to use to transfer food, in convenient pieces, into their mouths with the minimum of trauma to witnesses.

We may be happy when we're eating, but we are certainly not at our prettiest. If you want to make a good impression on someone, you will find it easier to look dignified when drinking a pint of stout than when tackling a plate of tagliatelle. This is the kind of thing that people should bear in mind – agonise over, even – when they are going on that crucial first date.

Of course, some of the best people in the world, in the widest and truest sense of the word, have no table manners to speak of. And you would be well advised to wear rain gear when sitting down to eat with them.

But there's no doubt that proper table manners are a social advantage, and if you want your children to shine in business or the professions, they may find it easier if they don't remove their earwax with a table knife while making a speech through a gobbet of half-chewed veal liver.

The naming of meals

Everyone has breakfast. Some people have morning coffee. Others have elevenses. Almost everybody has lunch, while only a very few (and usually only on embossed invitations) are invited to luncheon.

Some have tea – as in tea and sandwiches and a spot of cake – in the afternoon, but usually if they are exhausted from shopping and manage to stagger into a suitably old-fashioned hotel for resuscitation. Otherwise, this kind of tea is confined to those remnants of the upper classes who still have the time, the money and the staff to indulge.

Many more have tea in the sense of their evening meal. This notion has entered the collective psyche of the RTÉ newsroom, which frequently announces that some grisly event occurred 'around teatime'. When is that? Six o'clock? Surely most people wouldn't be home from work at that stage? Does it mean seven o'clock? And if you're commuting from Mullingar to Dublin, what time would you get back for your 'tea'?

The members of the Fine Gael parliamentary party who resisted the heave against Enda Kenny in the summer of 2010 were widely described as men (men, note) who have their dinner in the middle of the day. This would suggest that they are all agricultural workers, because it's only in the farming community that the tradition of the main meal at lunchtime persists. And for sensible reasons.

But it's interesting that the main meal is described as 'dinner' whether taken in the middle of the day or at any other time.

For some, supper is the main meal of the day, taken in the evening at around seven o'clock and being, in effect, dinner. I know this is getting complicated. Just concentrate.

The kind of people who have supper as their main meal of the day call it that because they think of dinner as being a grander and more formal affair, often involving guests. For most people, of course, supper is what you have directly before going to bed. But this practice is dying out, as we come to realise that your tummy needs a rest while you sleep.

So, if someone invites you to supper, you may have to think hard. Are you being asked to an evening meal, probably in the kitchen, served with a minium of fuss? Or will you end up with a couple of Goldgrain biscuits and a glass of warm milk?

Ice cream

I belong to a generation that is, on average, rather low on tonsils. In my time, if a child was not watched carefully, it would have its tonsils whipped out by a passing surgeon before you could say 'Forceps, nurse'.

I came close to having my own tonsils ripped from their moorings thanks to a few sore throats, but I was spared in the end, possibly by simply getting better or acquiring other, less fashionable ailments. My friends and cousins were not so lucky. They were whisked off to Temple Street or Harcourt Street and would awake, after the terrible deed, to find that there was one compensation for their loss. They would be fed ice cream until their poor little throats had healed. And quite possibly jelly too. Especially if they were private patients.

We were extremely patriotic about ice cream. In our view, the stuff they had across the water was very inferior and, indeed, some British ice cream of those days had never seen even a teaspoon of dairy produce. But no, what bothered us was the colour. Ice cream was meant to be snow white, surely? What was this yellow stuff to which English friends and relations were addicted?

Visiting English kids soon learned to keep their mouths shut about the ghostly confection that made them feel, even more than the sight of green pillar boxes, that they were in an alien land. If they didn't, they would feel the full force of juvenile patriotism, in the form of a blow for Irish ice cream.

Much as I subscribed to this slightly chauvinistic view

of the ice cream debate, I knew a terrible secret. My mother occasionally made ice cream: the real thing, with, er . . . actual cream. The colour of cream was no trouble, of course. But, as my mother explained very patiently, you couldn't just freeze sweetened cream. No, you had to turn the cream into a kind of custard, and then freeze it.

The custard needed eggs, of course, and the resulting ice cream – *real* ice cream – was yellow! I consumed this stuff in private, partly for reasons of patriotism, but largely because it was so rich, and so good.

Of course, at this stage ice cream was simple stuff. You bought it in 'bricks' of one pint's capacity and sliced it so that it could be sandwiched between two wafers. It came in three sorts: vanilla, raspberry ripple and Neapolitan. Neapolitan was a curious thing, and as closely related to Naples as I am. It involved three colours: white (vanilla) in the centre, with pink (strawberry) and brown (chocolate) flanking it on either side.

Then there were ice cream birthday cakes. I've no idea where they came from, but they were the must-have accessory when I was lacking a few front teeth.

That was as exotic as it got. These were the days before the Vienetta dawned upon us, when Romantica was still beyond our imagination. The days of innocent ice cream . . .

Arctic Roll

When I was growing up, we tended to lag behind Britain in certain respects. We were not nearly as good as letting the trade unions create a state of near-anarchy, for example. And we also lacked access to Arctic Roll.

If you have forgotten, this delicacy of the icebox is a cylinder of vanilla ice cream coated with a kind of raspberry jam and then encased in a jacket of sponge, not unlike a layer of industrial Swiss roll. It took a long time to come to Ireland, and I became aware of it only when I was a student.

In fact, Arctic Roll is a whole year older than I am. It was invented by a Czech lawyer by the name of Velden, and the first factory to produce it was opened on the Sussex coast in 1958. I have no idea why it took so long to come to Ireland. Were we just too poor to want such unwonted luxury?

I occasionally used to house-sit for my sister in those days and, forced to cater for myself, my diet consisted mainly of Findus Crispy Pancakes and Arctic Roll. Both of these fine products eventually went off the market, thanks, we are told, to increasing affluence and sophistication. Crispy Pancakes, created in Britain in the 1970s, managed to get to Ireland before Arctic Roll. Very odd.

It seems that we reached a point where we looked askance at such creations of the food industry. But we have come back, tails between our legs, chastened by the new economic reality, asking to have these simple pleasures returned to us. And they have been.

When Bird's Eye relaunched Arctic Roll a couple of years ago, they spewed out 250 miles of the thing in the first few months. Reports in the trade press cited 'nostalgia' and a desire for 'comfort food' as the impetus behind the success of the relaunch.

Hugh Fearnley-Whittingstall, before he was sent off to school at Eton, and many years before he set up River Cottage, adored Findus Crispy Pancakes. So much so that when he had reached man's estate and acheieved considerable celebrity status, he tried to recreate the Crispy Pancake – with what success I cannot say.

But the power of television being what it is, Findus was inspired to relaunch the Crispy Pancake, and to introduce some new flavours, as a kind of nod to how much more sophisticated and well travelled we are these days. Facebook was used to test the public's enthusiasm for the launch of the chicken-curry flavour. Not surprisingly, it was unleashed on a grateful public.

Findus now has lobster thermidor, lamb tagine and butternut squash flavours in their Crispy Pancake armoury, along with the three originals: minced beef, three cheeses and, my favourite, chicken with bacon and sweetcorn.

OK, I will happily admit that I have not actually eaten a Findus Crispy Pancake since the 1980s, but I still relish the idea of that crisp exterior giving on to the flexible membrane of pancake and then the scaldingly hot, molten interior. I think this was probably the last time that I would have been susceptible to the idea of 'food production technology' being entirely a good thing.

For some peculiar reason, I tend to bracket Crispy Pancakes, Jaffa Cakes and Arctic Roll together. Maybe it's because they all belong to that frustrating category of Don't Bother Trying to Make This at Home. That's where the technology comes in.

The Jaffa Cake, essentially a cake-like disc designed to be pre-stale, if you see what I mean, and therefore incapable of getting much worse, topped with a kind of marmalade jelly and not-terribly-good dark chocolate, is much more than the sum of its parts. Those three less-than-yummy elements come together and create something well worth eating.

People can be terribly sniffy about Findus Crispy Pancakes and talk of Hugh Fearnley-Whittingstall having 'sold out' to Findus. Well, I hope he's cut some sort of deal with them for having rekindled the public's interest in this icon of the 1970s orange-and-avocado-themed kitchen. And Nigel Slater has described Arctic Roll as tasting of 'frozen carpet'. There are those, even, who say that Jaffa Cakes are not biscuits at all, within the meaning of the act.

But all three are frivolous and fun, and gave me a lot of pleasure over the years. I don't like the idea of living in a world that has become too sophisticated for such things – so that's one silver lining within the recessionary cloud.

Swiss roll

I can't understand how a family like mine, with a superb home baker in our midst, ate so many Swiss rolls in the 1960s. I can only assume that my poor mother needed a rest.

Of course, to me they were exotic and, in a sense, superior to what came out of the oven at home. They came from a factory and, did I but know it, those fillings came from a laboratory.

There was a snow-white substance that went with the 'chocolate'-flavoured Swiss roll, and there was a yellow one, with a texture not unlike Brylcreem, that went into the lemon version.

It was as if the manufacturers wanted to make their Swiss rolls to be as different as possible from any wholesome thing that could come out of a domestic kitchen. They were revolting, and they probably still are. But I didn't realise that at the time. Never mind the taste, my subconscious was telling me. Feel the novelty. And I, being well under the age of twelve at the time, listened to my inner voice of indiscriminate greed.

The '99'

Bog-standard vanilla ice cream and Cadbury's Flake are all very well in their own way, but when combined they amount to more than the sum of their parts. I had my first '99' from McCarthy's newsagents in Drumcondra around the time that the livery of CIÉ buses changed from green to a fetching combination of navy and cream. If pressed, I'd say that this was in 1967.

The odd thing is that the '99' seems to have been invented long before then, but I distinctly remember it as something new and freshly minted – at least in the minds of Irish children – not long after we had all celebrated the fiftieth anniversary of the Easter Rising.

Nobody, not even Cadbury's, knows why the '99' was so called, but they do say that they started making sawn-off Flakes, suitable for serving with ice cream, as early as 1930. At first, they were made for the Italian ice cream vendors of Scotland and Northern England and were put into ice cream sandwiches. By the time the cornet – or cone, as we would say – became popular and was being filled with 'soft serve' ice cream of the sort we know today, Cadbury's was selling specially shortened Flakes in big boxes for the trade.

A '99' was a bit of a treat, an extravagance. The ice cream van that visited our bit of suburbia did a much cheaper cone, which had red and green syrup, of a particularly vile kind, drizzled on top to take the bare look off things. I can remember that cloying, clinging taste as if it was yesterday.

The great affinity that the Cadbury's Flake has for ice

cream is, of course, easily celebrated at home, but there is a superior combination that is, quite possibly, the food of angels. You crumble your Flake on top of your scoops of ice cream and then slice, thinly, a very ripe banana on top. Or you can smash a Crunchie and use that instead. This is the road to diabetes if you indulge too often. But, my goodness, it's hard to resist on occasion.

Schpring schprong

Jacob's were great biscuit-makers, and they were pioneers in many ways too. I think they were the first to create biscuits involving marshmallow. They did this in the closing years of the nineteenth century – a time when everyone seemed to believe that the future meant Science and Progress.

The marshmallow biscuits that were invented in Peter Street, just opposite the old Adelaide Hospital, caught, in their names, the zeitgeist. One was called Kimberley, after the diamond mining town in what became Rhodesia, and then Zimbabwe. The other very cheekily borrowed its name from that of Gilbert & Sullivan's smash-hit operetta, *The Mikado*.

The Mikado was, and still is, a rectangular biscuit covered with marshmallow and a stripe of raspberry jam down the centre, the whole lot enveloped in a kind of snowstorm of dessicated coconut. It was introduced to the world in 1888, three years after *The Mikado* (or *The Town to Titipu*) opened at the Savoy Theatre in London.

Five years later, in 1893, the Kimberley first saw the light of day. It comprised, as it still does, a round of marshmallow sandwiched between two discs of relatively soft ginger-flavoured biscuit, of the sort that adheres to your teeth within a nanosecond of your taking a bite. And, very importantly, the exposed surface of the marshmallow, around the rim of the composite biscuit, is encrusted in sugar crystals. This, it seems, was originally a nod to Kimberley's jewels.

In the fullness of time, Jacob's had the inspired idea of dipping Kimberley's in chocolate – a process which not only made the whole thing tastier but also seemed to add substance and stature. Well, that and the individual foil wrappers which were used for a while after the launch.

As to the *schpring* and the *schprong*, these words were coined for a 1970s advertising campaign. I think they did a good job of emphasising the rather jolly, bouncy character of these distinctively Irish biscuits. The phrase '*schpring-sch-prongs*' is, in effect, a generic catch-all term for all three. I can't imagine why Jacob's bothered to launch the Coconut Cream in 1935. This is virtually indistinguishable from the Mikado except for the fact that its base is round. Coconut creams have their adherents (often literally, as the marsh-mallow is remarkably adhesive) but they don't seem to evoke such strong emotions as Mikados. And many a Mikado aficionado (so to speak) wouldn't thank you for a coconut cream. Me? I remain perfectly neutral: anything that contains coconut is fine in my book.

Baileys

Life in the 1970s was not cool. Take my word for it. But sometimes life in the 1970s seems quite close to me. There's something about memory that filters out the floral shirts, the wide lapels, the flares and the Hillman Avengers. But, of course, it was another world. No mobile phones. No internet. No computers smaller than the average house. A pocket calculator cost a month's salary, and the fax machine was still at the conceptual stage and seen only on *Tomorrow's World*. If I need further evidence of the distance between now and then, all I have to do is get out the DVDs of *Life on Mars*.

One of my children, having noticed that the cast of *Life on Mars* spend a great deal of their time in the pub, wondered if alcohol was a lot cheaper in 1973, when the series is set, than it is now. Well, I don't know. I suggested that, perhaps in those days (when I was thirteen, and not a consumer of alchol) people didn't have a lot else to do. And then it struck me that, at that stage, Gilbey's of Ireland were only a year away from creating a whole new kind of drink.

Baileys Irish Cream, a rather sickly beige liquid, was, according to legend, created in a research-and-development laboratory, somewhere in London's Soho, in the latter half of 1974. Bailey's passed the billion-bottle mark in 2007.

At a time when DCI Gene Hunt and his ilk regarded drink as a pint of Double Diamond (where is it now?) or a large Scotch, the boffins were creating a form of alcohol that would change the face of drinking forever. And Bailey's did just that.

Let's face it – and we have more difficulty in admitting this than the Manchester coppers of 1973 – Baileys is a female drink. This is not to say that there are countless women who would rather drink Brasso – which looks uncannily like Baileys in a certain light – but the simple fact is that when the first Irish cream liqueur was created, there were precious few 'hard' drinks that appealed to the feminine palate.

Wine did, of course, but wine was Blue Nun in those days: a sweet, mawkish blend of the cheapest German whites. And there was a brand of so-called sherry called Amicardo which, according to the TV commercial, was 'specially blended for the Irish palate' – i.e. sweet and flabby.

There was a serious gap in the market. In those days, the female taste in alcohol tended towards the sweet and mildly alcoholic. Remember Babycham? Harvey's Bristol Cream? See what I mean? Our grandmothers would probably remember port and lemon but, if they were respectable, they would have regarded this blameless if rather disgusting concoction as being confined to women of so-called easy virtue. In 1974, if you excluded Dubonnet (which, frankly, most people did), there was little else to appeal to what the marketing men (and yes, they were all men) saw as the female palate.

And so Bailey's was born. To be sure, there were sweet drinks on the market. Liqueurs were much bigger then than they are now, and Irish Mist, which was in effect a kind of Irish Drambuie but with better marketing, was a roaring success that consumed such huge amounts of rather basic Irish whiskey that it became, in time, essential to the country's distilling industry. But there was room for something more.

The history of Baileys Irish Cream is shrouded in mystery and legend. This owes a great deal to the inventors' natural reluctance to share with others their discovery of how to emulsify cream and whiskey.

Actually, there was no mystery about the basic process, which involved getting the spirit and the fat to blend; the trick was to get the emulsion to remain stable. The scientists managed to achieve stability that lasted for more than two years. Even better, they found a way to make the whiskey stop the cream from oxidising. In other words, it refused to go rancid, which is what fats do when exposed to the air, or even when kept stoppered in a bottle.

Whatever it was called – probably some dull combination of numbers and letters – when it was still in the lab, the new concoction, later to be marketed as Baileys Irish Cream, had the potential to become the biggest-selling liqueur in the world. And that's exactly what it is today.

The success of Baileys Irish Cream is beyond question. Why this should be so is open to debate. But let's consider for a moment how significant it is. And in an era when Irish success stories have been ten a penny (at least until recently), let's remember that it had its genesis, and its early successes, in a time when the country was, by and large, an economic basket case. Baileys Irish Cream, bizarre as it may seem, provided one of the first examples of Ireland being able to produce what the world wanted to buy – and to counterfeit, wherever possible.

Imitation may be the sincerest form of flattery, but counterfeiting means you really have it made. All around the globe, unscrupulous businesses have been either copying the distinctive Baileys packaging or producing versions that are so close to the original as to be indistinguishable at first glance. Baileys have a 'black museum' of examples, and take great pains to track down and prosecute offenders.

Almost 4.5 percent of Irish milk production goes into Baileys – that is, the output of some 40,000 cows on 1,500 farms, most of them in the south-east. It takes a lot of cattle-power to fill almost 7 million bottles of Baileys every year.

So, what's the appeal? Well, with an alcohol content of 17 percent abv, it's in the same league as sherry, and therefore mild in moderation. The flavour is unashamedly sweet – and owes more to chocolate and caramel than it does to whiskey. The cream delivers a satin-smooth texture which competiors find very hard to imitate.

But who drinks Baileys? Well, if the TV commercials are to be believed, Baileys drinkers are young, well-heeled, urban and sophisticated – and equally divided between male and female. Which is rubbish. The truth is that Baileys appeals to a female constituency, and essentially to people who rarely drink alcohol. It could hardly be any other way, given how it tastes.

Baileys Glide, a long drink designed to take some of the alcopop market, must have seemed like a good idea at the time, but it didn't work. The poor deluded youngsters who buy alcopops tend to drink more than is good for them, and the Baileys brand, however the advertisers try to persuade us otherwise, is simply not a youthful one.

In the contemporary world, it's refreshing to see a brand defy the marketing gurus' edict that the youth market is all that matters. Baileys is a clever idea. With a wholly invented name (for 'R. & A. Bailey', read Diageo, the drinks multinational), and by tapping into the vaguest notion of Irish dairy and distilling traditions, it has seduced a huge market worldwide: the millions of people who don't really like alcohol but feel obliged to have a little every now and then.

I bet the inventors of Baileys Irish Cream didn't intend to capture that market, but I'm equally sure that Diageo are delighted that they have managed, perhaps unwittingly, to do so. It just shows that a brand doesn't have to be young and cool to succeed. Baileys is as young and cool as a twin-set and pearls but, by golly, it's huge.

Bird's Custard

Bird's Custard isn't what it used to be. When I first tucked into it, many years ago, it was a more vivid shade of yellow than it is now. I suspect that this is because my generation was brought up on azo dyes and E numbers. A little bit of Sunset Yellow never did us any harm. Or none that we know of. Yet.

Today, Bird's is a kind of pastel yellow – the sort of colour, in fact, which I have in mind for our hallway. Not too dramatic, but bright enough to enhance the light levels. But back to the custard.

The pedants will point out that Bird's isn't custard at all within the meaning of the act. Custard is, strictly speaking, milk or cream, or a mixture of the two, which has been thickened by adding eggs, and heating. In the amateur kitchen, by contrast, custard is understood to come in powder form, in tins.

The history is significant. Mrs Alfred Bird was allergic to eggs but partial to a little custard. Her loving husband set about producing an eggless custard. He had to find a way of thickening the milky mixture; he hit on the idea of using cornflour, which, like arrowroot, thickens any liquid upon the application of heat.

Mr Bird added colour, vanilla extract and various other items (which now come under the rather vague heading of 'ingredients' on the label). His wife was delighted. The product was created in 1837, and by the end of the nineteenth century Bird's had a vast factory in Birmingham making custard – as well as blancmange powder, jelly crystals and baking powder.

The brand has changed hands on several occasions but is one of the most easily recognised ones. In Britain, 99 percent of consumers know Bird's custard powder – and, latterly, various instant and ready-to-pour versions.

If you ever visit the rather dull Oxfordshire town of Banbury, where I once had to go for a job interview, you may notice that the place smells of Bird's custard. This is because Banbury is currently the *fons et origo* of all the Bird's Custard powder consumed in the world.

In my view, Bird's is a much better choice than the real thing when it comes to making a proper, old-fashioned sherry trifle. And it goes amazingly well with blackberries. But it is perhaps at its best with a traditional Irish apple pie. When I was small, it was good even with ice cream (but had to be consumed rapidly). I have known people to add drinking-chocolate powder to Bird's in order to produce a form of chocolate custard, but this, for me, is a bridge too far.

Bird's may be less violently coloured now that it's tinted with harmless, natural annato (the stuff that's used in making red Cheddar), but the taste remains constant. Most people make it far too thick. The ideal consistency for Bird's custard is not far off that off Heinz tomato soup: it should be somewhere between drinkable and eatable.

You may regard Bird's custard as bland – and it's certainly very suitable for nursing invalids back to health – but it can be dangerous. Thirty years ago, a cloud of custard dust exploded at Bird's Banbury factory. So don't throw it in the air and smoke at the same time.

Buns and the white heat of technology

It was the same with sweaters. You see, my mother was a very enthusiastic knitter, and much of what I wore as a child was home produced.

My jumpers were, I suppose, the kind of things that would now cost a fortune. Artisan knitwear, so to speak, is very fashionable and desirable now. But when I was small, it just suggested that you couldn't afford to buy stuff in shops. At least, that's the way it seemed to the under-tens of the late 1960s. Oh yes, stuff from shops was *real*; stuff that was produced at home was rather inferior. The same, needless to say, went for cakes, but at least you were spared the shame of having to wear home-made Victoria sponge in public.

Around the time that Harold Wilson was making speeches about the white heat of technology across the water in Britain, my parents started to buy the occasional commercial cake. I still have no idea why. I doubt it was to placate me. They were old enough to know better – to realise that what came out of the kitchen was always going to be better than something fresh from the factory.

And I doubt it was even for convenience. My parents belonged to a generation that distrusted the whole concept of making things easy. The word 'convenient' might be applied to bus stops or hardware stores, but not to food.

Anyway, the first mass-produced cake I can recall was a Swiss roll that contained a yellow substance which, if it had been made by a real cook, would have been butter-cream icing. I don't know what it was made from, but it was flavoured with synthetic pineapple. This combination of flour, fat and chemicals was lapped up by me, and consumed with rather less relish by the rest of the family. The hot, strong tea probably took the harm out of it.

The Swiss roll came in a brightly coloured box. But there were other boxes – white ones tied with string – that betokened something very different. These were cakes from the shop, yes, but from a proper baker's shop, not a factory.

If I was in luck, such a container would be opened to reveal eclairs. These were always a source of wonder: one of the few things that my mother didn't cook was choux pastry. The crisp shell of choux, the huge amount of cream, and the brilliantly appropriate chocolate topping all conspired to produce something that made me hop from foot to foot in breathless anticipation.

Actually, the acme of choux-pastry perfection in those days came from Fuller's in Grafton Street, which went the way of all flesh many years ago. Fuller's did a kind of choux ball, filled it with cream and – here's the trick – covered it in a very sweet form of coffee-flavoured satin icing. These blonde bombshells were the stuff of dreams.

Fuller's was a cake shop, and I think it may have been a café of sorts too. But they also did very chewy fruit sweets which were similar, but far superior, to Opal Fruits. But Opal Fruits always had the edge because they were restricted to our separated brethren in the United Kingdom. However, I digress . . .

I never shared by father's enthusiasm for Bewley's

cherry buns, but I regularly tucked in to the almond version. These bready things had – and still have, as far as I know – a good thick dollop of marzipan swirled in before baking. I can still remember the lovely contrast of cold, salty butter spread on the sweet, nutty centre. There was one confection from Bewley's, however, after which I lusted. This was the mini-trifle (sponge, jam, custard, maybe even a suspicion of booze, topped with whipped cream), which came in little individual containers fashioned from waxed card. When I was eight, this was probably as good as food got.

While there was always home-made fruitcake to hand, brack was bought in. And always from Bewley's. Stray bracks would occasionally turn up, bought from lesser bakeries, and they were never in the same league. At Hallowe'en, even the rings were better from Bewley's.

I learned very early on that while fresh brack is very good – having that open texture which is delivered by the yeast working its magic – it's even better when it has matured a little and you toast it. This has the effect of making it a bit crisp, obviously, but it also caramelises and intensifies the flavour of the raisins, sultanas and candied peel. Not that I would have recognised the word 'caramelised' in those days. But, had I heard it, it would have intrigued me. Anything to do with caramel . . . But that's another day's work.

When I was about thirteen, I discovered that the staff of life was not so much bread but a yeast bun with cream and a dollop of that intensely red stuff that passes for jam (or maybe even, God help us, 'coulis' these days) in the world of commercial baking.

These buns, which I bought daily after alighting from the bus home from school, were showered in icing sugar, so that my black blazer would end up looking rather snow-flecked.

By that stage, I had realised that home cooking was far superior to anything you could buy in a shop or a takeaway (even Kentucky Fried Chicken, which was very new and quite alluring; I mean, *how* many herbs and spices?).

And I suppose when you come to that conclusion, and if you're lucky enough to be very well fed at home, shop-bought stuff becomes a kind of guilty pleasure. Those rather terrible post-school buns taught me that guilt and pleasure *can* go together. And when they do, the mixture is quite heady.

Seedy cake

Caraway seeds, like Marmite and the gherkins in McDonald's hamburgers, evoke strong emotions, mostly of distaste. I know very few people, apart from my wife Johann, who likes that distinctive and frankly rather *mittel* European flavour.

She was fortunate in that she was brought up in a caraway-tolerant househould. I grew up hearing about caraway as a frightful natural substance which should be avoided in much the same way as the *News of the World* and Maoist students.

At the height of my adolescent gardening phase, I enjoyed growing stuff that was unusual or hard to find. I tried caraway one year. It developed pungent foliage and, after a warm, dry summer, fleshy green seeds, which, when dried, could have gone into a basic sponge mixture to make caraway seed cake, or 'seedy cake'. Instead, I munched them fresh and never looked back.

Caraway is a great help to the digestion (which is why the liqueur Kummel is so good after over-indulging), and I love its utterly distinctive smell and taste. It's not like anything else that I can name. Is there the faintest suggestion of dill, or do I think that because gripe water traditionally contained extracts of both of these herbs?

Caraway seed cake is delightful, but we usually divide the sponge mixture, with its payload of what looks distressingly like dessicated mouse droppings, between bun cases. And we sometimes roast potatoes with caraway seeds – a very Germanic thing to do. As is adding a few to red cabbage as you cook it slowly for Christmas.

My parents would be horrified.

Angel Delight

Oh how I loved Angel Delight. Particularly the strawberry and butterscotch flavours. They tasted so correct, so pure, so creamy, so wholesome.

My parents, like most of their generation, were quite accepting of technology as a form of progress. True, they didn't quite approve of television, and believed that the output from Montrose could be, and frequently was, corrupting. They didn't approve of building roads, because they thought it would make it just too easy for people to go gadding about. And as for advances in pharmaceuticals, they were all very well, but don't mention the Pill!

Bird's Angel Delight was technology in a bowl, introduced as the Ford Anglia became the Ford Escort and the restaurant at the top of the Post Office Tower made its first revolution. Angel Delight was cool, in every sense. All you had to do was pour the powder into some ordinary milk and whisk, whereupon it was transformed into a deliciously creamy dessert. And my mother regarded it as a good way of getting milk into me.

Bird's, who subsequently sold the brand to Premier Foods, launched the first Angel Delight in the early summer of 1967 – which coincided happily with my eighth birthday. It was a 'strawberries and cream' version; I can remember being pleasantly surprised that something that came out of a packet could taste so like the real thing. And the colour – God knows what it came from – was right too. It wasn't shocking, Barbie pink. It was *wholesome* pink.

Friends recall having Angel Delight turned into ice

lollies by indulgent but milk-conscious parents. I never had one of those. By the time my children were born, Angel Delight was well out of fashion, and frozen Petits Filous were more in tune with the kind of parents to be found in leafy south Dublin suburbia.

Angel Delight's fightback started just before the millennium, with an advertising campaign featuring Wallace and Gromit. Personally, I'm a sucker for anything endorsed by this pair, but even I wouldn't fancy popcorn- or candyfloss-flavoured Angel Delight – which came with the relaunch. Nor did the public; now the range is back to the original line-up of strawberry (yum), butterscotch (yum), banana (not as bad as it sounds), raspberry (fine) and chocolate (no thanks). I have a feeling that Angel Delight is here to stay this time.

All sorts of lick-rish

I've often wondered why so many people call liquorice 'lick-rish'. Perhaps it's because we encounter the word in early childhood and can't quite get our tongues around it. Not that it appears to appeal to the average child much anyway.

When I was little, liquorice came in various forms. There were the long black strands that were known as bootlaces and – this shows how much the world has changed in the meantime – liquorice fashioned into the shape of a curved smoking pipe with red candy bits representing the burning tobacco. And, of course, there was a liquorice tube sticking out of every sherbert fountain. But I found the taste too strong, a bit too bitter despite the sweetness.

During my primary-school years, my friends and I tended to prefer liquorice-flavoured toffee, which, thanks to copious amounts of colouring, had the further benefit of turning your tongue jet black. The one I remember best was made by Lemon's in Drumcondra. I could always tell, on my way home from school, when they were making it because the air around the River Tolka would be beautifully scented with liquorice. The stuff really does have a lovely fragrance. I also remember liquorice toffee because it pulled out more of my milk teeth than you might imagine. There was always a surprising crunch before the taste of the toffee mingled with the salty flavour of blood.

The very vivid memory of that makes me shudder now that I'm a boring old grown-up. There was a very posh luxury version that was produced by Callard & Bowser, but it seems to have vanished. And it was just as good at informal and unexpected tooth-pulling.

True liquorice comes from the root of *Glychyrizza glabra*, a Mediterannean plant which I've grown on occasion just out of curiosity. It has rather attractive grey-green foliage, and if you crush the leaves you get a subtle scent that suggests a distant bag of liquorice allsorts.

The sort of liquorice that you get in the all-black liquorice allsorts is actually a combination of the juice of its root along with powdered sugar and vegetable starch. In its unadulterated form it has a very strong taste and, oddly enough, is one of the sweetest substances in nature.

There was a time when you could easily buy lengths of liquorice root for chewing (or for giving to teething children) but these days you will have to go to a good health-food shop. Traditionally, liquorice has been used to treat coughs and colds and to help heal gastric ulcers. It's very soothing on the gut and has fairly significant anti-inflammatory powers, apparently. And as anyone who has gone to town on a packet of Bassett's best knows, liquorice is a very thorough laxative. If I had known this as a child, in the days when there was a wholesale obsession with bowels, I would have campaigned for a liquorice ration in place of the dreaded Senokot.

You will still see bottles and drawers in old-fashioned chemist shops (like Lane McCormack's in Monkstown) labelled '*Glychh. Glab*', a reminder of the time when not just the Roman Catholic Church did everything through Latin – pharmacists did too.

Liquorice, as it turns out, is not as innocent as it may

appear. It has long been known that it tends to increase blood pressure, but until recently it was thought that you would need to eat a vast amount of it to be affected. Not so, according to a report in *Nature* a few years ago, which quotes an Icelandic study. A few handfuls of liquorice allsorts can be enough. As a result, it should supposedly be avoided by people with hypertension and those on digoxin-based drugs.

Pontefract cakes – little discs of liquorice – occasionally made their way into our household, but I gave them a wide berth. They seemed to be the purest and most austere form of liquorice, the sort that only deluded adults could bring themselves to munch.

They are still made in the small Yorkshire town of that name (which some people pronounce 'Pomfret'). Although they carry the name of the inventor, one Mr Dunill, the brand is German-owned these days. Actual liquorice cultivation in England died out during the last century, and these days it tends to be grown in southern Europe and Russia. In the old days, liquorice was always known as Spanish root: originally, it seems to have been brought from Spain by monks. How it ended up being grown commercially in the damp and chilly climate of Yorkshire rather than, say, Surrey, I don't know, nor am I sure if there is any evidence of it having been grown here in Ireland.

Speaking of Surrey, that *enfant terrible* of the Home Counties, Richmal Crompton's William Brown, was, with his friends the Outlaws, something of a liquorice aficionado. So fond of it were they that they shook pieces of the stuff in bottles of water in order to produce a cloudy beverage. I was always tempted to try, but never got around to it. One thing is sure, though. The chewing of liquorice, like pipe-smoking and hat-wearing amongst men, is pretty much a thing of the past.

I have overcome my childhood revulsion towards real liquorice and quite fancy the odd bag of allsorts, in which the sugary fondant seems to take the edge off the black stuff. I'm particularly keen on the orange ones, and I've always had a fascination with the little round jellies covered in tiny blue balls. They taste of aniseed to me. But then again, aniseed and liquorice are quite similar in flavour.

I've had liquorice in gravy – sorry, *jus* – where it didn't seem to do any harm, and I was once served liquorice ice cream with a lavender biscuit, which was wickedly lovely. So much so that I keep promising myself to imitate the dish at home.

Oh, and by the way, if you say 'lick-rish' and want to stop and turn over a new leaf, just forget the spelling. Think of it as 'lick – er – iss'. Simple, isn't it?

Biscuits

There was always a certain frugality about plain biscuits – the sort you got during the year rather than at Christmas. And the plainest of them all was Marietta, which can still be bought. Before they invented the rather less tasty H2-receptor antagonists, Marietta was, in combination with milk, the front-line therapy for duodenal ulcers. And that was until Tagamet was introduced in the late 1970s.

The thing to do with Mariettas, of course, was to make sandwiches of them with a generous spread of butter. When you pressed the two Mariettas together, you got tiny worms of butter extruded through the holes. That was fun.

Rich Tea was similar but a shade less frugal. But still decidedly plain. Though less plain, of course, than Lincoln Creams, which were characterised by their plentiful crop of biscuity pimples. They were, and still are, a kind of shortbread – but not the sort that came in tins from Walkers in Scotland with oodles of butteriness. That kind of shortbread biscuit belonged in the 'luxury' category.

Bourbons never greatly appealed to me. Their half-hearted chocolatiness made them, for me, not quite a biscuit within the true meaning of the term. Then there were sandwich biscuits with a kind of yellow cream filling, one with a shortbread type of exterior, the other owing more to the plainer Marietta tradition. For all I know, they may still be out there.

Morning Coffee is still around – though probably in decline, now that biscuits have been elevated to dizzying heights of sophistication. But I always enjoyed the shockingly sweet icing, with its shiny, smooth surface and curiously granular interior texture. Again, the biscuit base was a variation on the plainest of Marietta themes, redeemed by a sugary icing with a suggestion of coffee and Muscovado.

Nice biscuits seem to have been named after the place in France – which seems odd. This biscuit is a celebration of dessicated coconut and a frugal plainness that puts it in much the same league as Mariettas. And much as I like coconut in every form, I can't claim that Nice biscuits are, er . . . particularly nice.

Shopping

When I was born, supermarkets were unknown in Ireland. Of course, they were not unheard of. They were known as far-off phenomena, more suited to the godless life of larger societies, but, nonetheless, sprinkled with a fair amount of fairy dust.

The first true supermarket was opened in New York City by an Irish-American named Cullen as far back as 1930. And in England, Sainsbury's opened their first self-service shop (nothing so vulgar as a supermarket) in 1950. Tesco opened its first supermarket, in Surrey, in 1956.

Here, things moved at a slower pace. Eventually, as the country marked the fiftieth anniversary of the Easter Rising, Dunnes Stores opened the first true supermarket, in 1966. It was at Cornelscourt in south County Dublin, and was ugly enough, with sufficient parking, to be the real thing.

Self-service had crept in already, of course. Ben Dunne had introduced this revolutionary idea to his first store, in central Cork, way back in the 1950s. And H. Williams (remember them?) were doing something similar by 1966. Their general manager, one Pat Quinn, wanted to open a full-blown supermarket at the new Stillorgan Shopping Centre, but permission was refused. So he left and started Quinnsworth. Dublin got two supermarkets in one year.

But at this stage, the only 'multiples' were old-fashioned chains with counter service, tradition and a certain pride. They seemed very superior to the brash, new, brightly lit supermarkets. The two best-known examples were the

Monument Creameries and Findlater's.

'The Monument', as it was called in our house, sold milk, butter and cheese. I remember it as being all tiles and white marble, with old-fashioned scales and fine displays of biscuits. It used also sell a form of cooking chocolate that came in lengths of what appeared to be a chunky brown dado rail.

The first Monument Creamery opened on Parnell Street in Dublin in 1919, just opposite the monument to Charles Stewart Parnell – hence the name. At the peak of its success there were thirty-six Monument Creameries around Dublin, but by 1968 the business was forced into liquidation. By now, the chain of grocers established by Findlater's more than a century before was struggling to survive. Despite a flirtation with self-service, which probably came about ten years too late, this fine old chain had disappeared before the decade was out. It belonged to an era when people – housewives, as they would have been then – went 'marketing'. This did not mean the dark arts of selling but the procurement of sustenance.

You would take a stout basket and do your rounds. Butcher, baker, creamery, greengrocer, fishmonger, general-provision merchant. And possibly a visit to your wines and spirits merchant – which was very often a pub. The basket, however, would be used to collect only the lighter items, or those that were required urgently. The rest would be delivered, very often by a youth on a specially contrived bicycle. The bike would have a vast basket to the front and the employer's name boldly written in white on black, but partially obscured by the rise and fall of bony knees. These young persons were referred to as 'messenger boys' –

something that my father used as a term of opprobrium, for any kind of uncouth young man, well after the species had become extinct.

Or your order was dispatched by van. We had our groceries delivered every week by Findlater's. This was rather a grand custom which was in inverse proportion to the family fortune, but it was splendidly convenient, especially as my somewhat Luddite parents didn't have a car. Every week, the Findlater's van would roll up, maroon red with gold lettering on the side, and as the driver unloaded the goods I would poke my head into the back to see what everyone else was getting. It tended to include a few dusty bottles with a flash of white paint on the sides, wrapped in straw protectors. I know now that this was vintage port, probably the 1955, and I see from an old list of theirs that this would have cost all of seventeen shillings for the Fonseca. Let me see. That would be the equivalent of . . . I was never good at maths . . . well, about a euro, anyway.

Those were the days. I blush to recall that, fired with childish curiosity, I once swiped a small bottle of Schweppes Indian Tonic Water from the back of the van; to this incident I ascribe both my aversion to gin and tonic and my strange compulsion to press half a crown into Alex Findlater's hand whenever I see him.

When Findlater's went the way of all flesh, my car-less parents had to find an alternative supplier of groceries. They settled upon yet another example of yet another species which would soon be extinct.

The charming O'Brien family had an independent self-service grocer's on Drumcondra Road which managed to cram into a remarkably small space all that the average family could possibly want in 1970 or thereabouts. I used to play with the O'Brien boys and can still remember the marvellous mixture of smells that created the distinctive aroma of the storeroom at the back of the shop. It involved candles, floor polish, Brillo pads and a suggestion of Parazone.

Dublin never had a Fortnum & Mason, but when I was small it had Smyth's of the Green – which was, considering that Dublin was an oversized village in those days, quite an achievement. By the time I knew it – and I knew it only very slightly, because my family were not exactly what you would call regular customers at this end of the food market – it was on its last legs. As far as I can gather, it closed down in 1974.

While Smyth's of the Green was merely the Fallon & Byrne of its day, it was a strange kind of day back then. In truth, the shop was a survival from more spacious days, when it would have done a brisk trade with the Viceregal Court and Dublin Castle. As the relics of oul' dacency declined, so did its fortunes. By the time I found myself browsing its fascinating shelves, it was an anachronism.

I remember Smyth's of the Green for three quite separate things. On a very early visit, I came across a tin of what I still swear were chocolate-covered bumble bees. I didn't quite approve of using bumble bees as food, but I decided that this was the most exotic thing I had ever encountered.

A few years later, I went in with my father to get some port for Christmas. This would have been just before it closed, and after it had joined up with the venerable Dublin wine merchants Thomson D'Olier. We bore away in triumph a bottle of Taylor's Late Bottled Vintage 1970, as far as I can remember.

And then there was the time we bought our first pepper grinder there (as discussed in the 'Pepper' section). Perhaps we could have tried Lipton's, which was on Grafton Street, close to the old Grafton Cinema. Although it was self-service by the time I knew it, Lipton's retained such a sense of superiority that it, and its few other braches in Ireland, closed by the end of the 1960s. The Lipton tea brand marched on, of course, and is now owned by Unilever.

The food shop that survives from my childhood is the remarkable Magill's delicatessen in Clarendon Street, a shop that was always full of mysterious and lovely smells, and still is. My father used to buy a strange form of pâté that came in tubes, like outsized toothpaste containers, from there.

In its time, Magill's was the most exotic thing in Dublin. Not only for its intriguing combination of fragrances but also for the loops of *saucisson* and salami which hang above your head. As a child, I was very keen to try them, but I was told firmly that I wouldn't like them. It turned out not to be true.

Jelly

I remember the first time I heard the word 'greengage'. I was very small, and I liked the sound of it. But I liked even more the vivid shade of green of the jelly that I was looking at. This, I was told, was greengage jelly.

I'm glad they didn't tell me that a greengage is a kind of plum. In those days I could take or leave plums, and I generally left them. Raw, stewed, in flans, whatever. But this green jelly, which was sweet and tart at the same time, was doing it for me.

For a long time in my very young life, I had a hazy notion that greengages and limes were more or less the same thing. Well, they were the right colour and, back in those days, I don't know where you would have had to go to see limes in the flesh, so to speak. Maybe Smyth's of the Green might have had them when they were in season. My closest contact was Rose's Lime Cordial, which was, well, green, and tasted a bit like my greengage jelly.

Jelly was not a consuming passion for me. I liked the colours, but it always had a lack of susbtance which made me feel let down somehow. And I could never understand the enthusiasm of some other children for jelly and ice cream. Those two textures together? No thanks.

But my father loved jelly until the day he died – almost literally. I remember him enjoying what must have been his last portion of the stuff when he was in Our Lady's Hospice in Harold's Cross. He could wax lyrical about jelly: he always recalled his very early encounters with it, and how it reminded him of the light coming through stained-glass windows. Jelly, for my father, was a reminder of the saints, ecclesiatical quiet, a faint smell of incense. This is in sharp contrast to Dame Nellie Melba, the Australian opera singer who was married to a very distant relation of ours. She once said: 'There are two things I like stiff. And one of them is jelly.'

Jelly merely reminded me of children's parties and the superiority of ice cream over not just jelly, but most food-stuffs.

There was one form of jelly – a kind of adapted and improved jelly – that was really good, however. So good, indeed, that I came to request it on birthdays and special occasions. The jelly was melted and allowed to come close to setting point, at which point lightly whipped cream was folded in. The proportions? About 70 percent jelly to 30 percent cream, as far as I can remember. And then the completed mixture – which would have started off as ruby-red jelly but which was now a shade of pink that might have shocked even Barbie – was left to set.

This combination was known in our household as 'stink puff', after one of Dr Spooner's famous gaffes. When he wanted some blancmange but couldn't remember the name of it, he indicated that he would like some of the 'stink puff'.

Roses

I was never a great fan of Hadji Bey's Turkish Delight, one of the delicacies of Cork – which was always referred to by a childhood friend of mine as 'Ah Bejaysus'. But I was attracted by the idea of the pink version – well, it was pinkish after you had shaken off all that icing sugar – because I had been told that it was flavoured with Turkish rosewater, which, in turn, would have been distilled from thousands of dark, sweetly scented blossoms.

I grew up with roses as a kind of constant backdrop, and by the time I was in my early teens I was even growing some myself – mainly the old-species varieties, which more than compensate for their short flowering season with their almost overpowering fragrance. I always preferred roses from the plant kingdom to Roses from Cadbury's.

In fact, I was very taken with the whole rose thing, having discovered a copy of Eleanour Sinclair-Rohde's book *The Scented Garden* in Greene's bookshop. I read its Elizabethan recipes for pot pourri and various other attractively smelly things with fascination. I even went so far as to try to find the likes of orris root and gum benjamin in what remained of Dublin's ancient 'medical halls' – those musty, dark-panelled old chemists' shops, with their huge carboys of coloured waters, and jars with labels all in mysteriously abbreviated Latin. Nowadays, of course, you could recreate the whole world of Elizabethan perfumery with stuff you can buy off the internet.

Were my parents bemused by this? Well, a little, but they liked that kind of thing. It was only when I had shot past puberty and decided to make rose-petal sandwiches that my mother started leaving cuttings from the *Catholic Herald* lying around the place. They all had a common theme: the 'evils' of homosexuality.

So that's what I got for making rose-petal sandwiches, encouraged by the same Eleanour Sinclair-Rohde: a mother's suspicions about my sexual orientation. Mind you, when I eventually acquired a girlfriend, I was told that she was the sort that got boys into trouble. I couldn't win.

I also have to report that rose-petal sandwiches are not very pleasant. No, I just wouldn't bother. But roses do have culinary applications, and you *can* capture some of that seductive scent in stuff that you can eat or drink.

A few years back, almost all of our strawberry crop went to feeding the local blackbirds. And when I say local, I mean every blackbird within about three miles. Hordes of them feasted on the fruits of the strawberry plants which I had imported, at some expense, from Marshall's of Cambridgeshire. They were a lovely variety called Marshmello, which have an old-fashioned strawberry taste and, just as important, a haunting strawberry fragrance. And the stalks come out easily. How often do you see that?

As a result of the measliness of our crop, I tried to enhance the flavour of the sort you buy on the side of the road (which seem to have improved over the past few years, I know not why). One trick I thought of trying was to make rose-petal cream. I dug out Joyce Molyneux's *The Carved Angel Cookbook*, she having run a famous Dartmouth restaurant which was more recently in the hands of John Burton-Race.

The Molyneux version was a disaster. It involves putting rose petals and cream in a blender and whizzing the two together. I ended up with rose-petal butter and a lot of beautifully coloured whey.

On the second attempt, I improvised. A generous handful of rose petals, cleared of any animal life, went into the blender with a dessertspoon of caster sugar, a squeeze of lemon juice and a few teaspoons of water. This produced an intensely fragrant and vaguely pink puree, which I folded into thickly whipped cream. After three hours in the fridge, it was dished up with fresh strawberries and was utterly delicious.

Now, the trick here is to choose your roses carefully. There's no point in using modern hybid teas, because they have little or no scent and the petals are too fleshy. You need proper old-fashioned roses, or the new English Roses from David Austin, which are bred to mimic the scent and form of the old varieties but flower for longer.

We have had varietal wines, so why not varietal rose-petal cream? Well, the combination I used was Zephyrine Drouhin and Fantin Latour. I'm tempted to try Rambling Rector, but its intense perfume smells more of hyacinths than roses. Could be interesting . . .

My daughter turned the rose-petal butter into icing for a Victoria sponge and filled it with what was left of the rose cream. Very sweet – but empty calories have rarely tasted so good.

Fizzing

Fizz was important. A sweet that fizzed, especially after some sedate sucking, was a proper sweet, a sweet with a bonus. Sherbet lemons still have a certain magic for me: I find it almost impossible not to bite before the end. A sherbet lemon, as any fule know (to quote Nigel Molesworth of *Back in the Jug Agane*), must be sucked until the fizz erupts from the core. Only then may you crunch the fizzed-out carcass of the sweet. Yes, there's an etiquette to most things.

There was a time when the tuck shop in my school did a roaring trade in Fizzle Sticks – lengths of extruded candy in rather girly pastel shades. But they had one mighty virtue. Bite them, chew them and they fizzed in the mouth, delivering a kind of generic, synthetic citrus flavour. No lunchtime was complete without a Fizzle Stick or two. They put a spring in your step.

And then there were Refreshers, a kind of fruity, mildly fizzy variation on the theme of Silvermints. But the best – and fizziest – of them all were Quenchers, little dense disks which, as soon as they hit your saliva, erupted into the production of carbon dioxide and the release of heaven knows what flavourings and colourings. Refreshers were for wimps. Quenchers took no prisoners.

Sherbet Fountains

I was never a huge fan of Sherbet Fountains, preferring to make my modicum of fizzy powder in a form which I think was called Dib Dabs.

Sherbet Fountains were paper cylinders containg the sherbet powder, and they had a hollow liquorice tube sticking out for sucking through. Sometimes the tube was solid – a terrible discovery. (In Britain, indeed, the tube was always solid in those days.) The liquorice was always a bit stale and, unless you could control the flow of your saliva in a way that many eight-year-olds have yet to master, the paper cylinder often ended up as papier mâché.

But some kids liked them, and they still do. The Sherbet Fountain brand (and I bet most of us didn't even know it was a brand) was sold for £58 million a few years ago. That's an awful lot of Sherbert Fountains.

The new owners decided to replace the paper cylinder with a rigid plastic one and, horror of horrors, the liquorice tube with a plastic, resealable one. This, it was explained, was in the interest of hygiene.

I don't know how many people succumbed to cholera or salmonella as a result of sucking a stale, sticky liquorice tube, but I bet the casualties are far outweighed by the hordes of children who boosted their immune systems in this simple and pleasurable way and who have now grown up to be nostalgic old codgers.

As it turned out, the people who shelled out over €60 million on the Sherbert Fountain, and messed up the original, got cold feet. You can once again suck the fizzy powder, if you are so inclined, through a hollow liquorice tube. This is one of those rare things: a victory for common sense.

Bobby Bar

P. G. Wodehouse was great at physical descriptions. I can't remember the character he was describing – I suspect it may have been Gussie Fink-Nottle – but he imagined Euclid seeing him and saying, more or less: 'Don't look now, but here comes a chap who demonstrates exactly what I was saying about a straight line having length and no breadth.'

Well, that was a pretty accurate description of me in the mid-1970s. Length (I was six foot two by the age of fifteen) and no breadth: my shoulders were narrower than my waist, which was a svelte twenty-eight inches. Finding jeans was a constant problem.

Anyway, it is amazing what the teenage frame can accommodate. I managed to remain somewhat sylph-like, albeit pretty tall at the same time, while consuming, *inter alia*, a can of Coke and a Bobby Bar whenever I was released from the classroom for what we cheerfully called 'lunch'.

Of Bobby Bars, there remains no trace. They were sold in Ireland, as far as I can gather, between roughly 1970 and 1975, and they came in a blue waxed-paper wrapper. It seems that they were made by the firm Urneys, and it is possible that they were named after a member of the Gallagher family, who owned Urneys until 1963. Bobby Gallagher, sadly, died young.

They were, in their essentials, a somewhat more proletarian (and therefore more attractive) version of the Bounty Bar (which in those days came, for no apparent reason, in not just an outer wrapper but a kind of cardboard gutter too). The similarity between the two bars lay in their high content of coconut – a substance which is almost as divisive as Marmite, caraway seeds and Enda Kenny. The difference – and their real attraction for me, at any rate – was the fact that in the Bobby Bar, the coconut was embedded in a toffee matrix so chewy that it could pull teeth. And of course, this magically attractive core was enrobed in chocolate.

The Bobby Bar was a true Irish original. I'm amazed that it was never copied in Britain, because it had an addictive quality for anyone who enjoys coconut – and chewing. The chewing, admittedly, required strongly anchored teeth and, given the astronomically high sugar content, a regular tooth-brushing habit.

I have since become keen on the Bounty Bar, especially the dark-chocolate variety. The moistness of the coconut flakes and the slightly bitter kick of the coating is very pleasant, but it's a grown-up kind of pleasure. Bounty ('they came in search of paradise') has since transmogrified into one of the very best confectionery/ice cream crossovers, riding roughshod over even the chilly manifestation of Malteser.

But could the Bobby Bar ever have made it into ice cream? No, I don't think so. Even on a warm day, a Bobby Bar could loosen fillings within seconds. Frozen, it would have been, to borrow a phrase from the Chistmas carol 'In the Bleak Midwinter', like iron.

Beanos

I think we can take devotion to Smarties as read. I mean, nothing comes close. I can even forgive them the fact that they no longer come in those excitingly huge tubes, or the little cardboard boxes with no tamper-proof seal. And the fact that the colours have changed a bit over the years. I would still quite like a mouthful of Smarties, to suck them slowly until they all go kind of off-white and the shells begin to crack and the chocolate starts to ooze out . . .

I think you probably get my drift.

But when I first found myself in thrall to the wonder of Smarties, an interloper appeared, a pretender to the Smarties crown. Beanos were a mercifully short-lived phenomenon in the late 1960s – a rather pathetic 'me-too' product inspired by the huge success of The Real Thing.

For me, they had the further disadvantage of being Irish – which meant that we had a patriotic duty to buy the charmless things. While the Smarties packaging was light and bright and engaging, the dominant theme on the Beanos box was the kind of brown more usually associated with the less-lively enclosed religious orders.

And the general dullness carried on from the packaging to the sweets themselves. They looked, at first glance, a little like Smarties, but they were a bit more domed and slightly more shiny. The real giveaway, however, was the colours. Beanos were too bright, too vivid. It was as if they protested just a bit too much.

But the worst thing about Beanos was the taste. While Smarties oozed the sensuously vanilla-scented chocolate in which Rowntree-Mackintosh (God be good to them) specialised, the Tallaght-produced Beanos tasted distinctly of peanuts. Not that there was any mention of peanuts on the packet, nor any stray bits in the chocolate.

They were rubbish. And the children of Ireland didn't buy them. Parents sometimes foolishly bought Beanos Easter eggs (a nightmare scenario for any self-respecting pre-teen chocolate lover in those days), but kids just didn't buy Beanos for themselves, and they gradually faded away.

Two-and-Two

I was a late convert to Urney's Two-and-Two bar, having always entertained a suspicion of Irish chocolate. This was due to my early exposure to Beanos (*qv*); I approached anything that was not made by either Cadbury's or Rowntree-Mackintosh with considerable caution and suspicion.

But one day, as I walked home from the bus stop after school, a friend of mine offered me a square of this almost unknown bar, and I was hooked. It was the combination of white vanilla fondant and a slightly grainier, caramel fondant, and – I'm not sure of this – dark chocolate underneath and milk chocolate on top that did it for me. And the squares were not like Cadbury's squares, which were all completely separate. This bar appeared to have channels running between them. A bit weird, really. The wrapper was exceptionally ugly: brown, cream and red.

The trouble is, the Two-and-Two didn't last long, so my memories of our brief romance are very hazy. But I do remember it as being very sweet.

Some of my contemporaries recall asking shopkeepers how much a Two-and-Two was, just in order to hear the answer 'fourpence'. Less than a shilling, that was. Oh, we made our own entertainment in those days.

Cream soda

I have been amazed to find that cream soda is known out-side Ireland, and in much the same form. This fizzy drink haunted my childhood, with its strangely unpleasant but hard-to-define flavour. I think my first encounter with it was when I was sick and it was being used to rehydrate me.

The flavour I now know to be vanilla; I'm at a loss to know how anyone thought that was a good idea. I'm assuming that the flavour was not derived from vanilla pods. The only excuse I can find is the suggestion that the cream soda was made expressly as a suitable liquid in which to float vanilla ice cream: a convention in parts of England in the early twentieth century.

In my childhood, it was always called 'American cream soda' – in much the same way as dingy pubs in small rural villages proclaimed themselves 'The American Bar' or dusty hairdressing salons in provincial towns would trum-pet the magic words 'late of New York'. And I seem to remember that there was a rather inferior selection of bis-cuits with the ludicrous moniker 'USA Assorted'.

Anyway, there are not many remembered flavours which make me gag, but this is one of them.

Fry's Chocolate Cream

My grandfather introduced me to Fry's Chocolate Cream during his declining years. His other pleasures during his final furlong included Sweet Afton cigarettes, a raw egg in sherry every morning, and a nightcap of Power's Three Swallows Whiskey (which he took in small and considered swallows, I should stress).

Nothing tastes quite like a Fry's Chocolate Cream bar, and I had no idea how sophisticated and grown-up it was the time I first munched one. No, not munched. You don't munch a bar like this. You *savour* it.

You savour it because the chocolate is dark and bitter and the filling is very sweet, but there's only just enough of it. Brought together by your teeth, these two elements react with each other to produce a taste that is reminiscent of neither: a kind of clean, comforting yet vaguely refreshing taste with just a touch of austerity.

I think I was six at the time, but I can still remember this utterly new taste as if it was yesterday.

Fig Rolls

You need to be above a certain age to remember Jim Figgerty. He was the mysterious, elusive figure at the centre of one of the most innovative Irish advertising campaigns of the late 1960s. The shadowy Mr Figgerty was eventually revealed to be the man who knew how to put the figs into Jacob's fig rolls. He was recently revealed, by the *Mayo News*, to have been one Patrick Griffin, an Irish tenor who toured the country with a tent.

A previous advertising campaign centred on the very pertinent question of how Jacob's managed to get the figs into their fig rolls. It is a reflection of the quiet times that were in it that this kind of teaser actually worked. Now, if you have never actually seen a fig roll, there's not much point in my attempting to describe one for you. Suffice it it to say that, way back in the innocent 1960s, it was a bit of a mystery how . . . well, how they got the figgy bit in the centre and the biscuity bit all around it, with no *seam*. If you follow.

In fact, the fig roll may have been one of the world's first extruded products, dating from well before plastics were given this treatment. Essentially, the fig filling is pumped out in the centre while the biscuit mixture is pumped out around the filling. The whole thing is then chopped up into biscuit-sized sections and baked quite slowly and at a relatively cool temperature – to get the soft biscuit texture, which goes so well with the yielding fig filling. The process allows the filling to merge imperceptibly with the shell, so to speak.

Fig rolls were a great innovation in their day, and they still command a loyal following, while also dividing opinion. There are those who loathe the seedy texture of figs in any form, but particularly in biscuits.

Fig rolls were invented by Jacob's and introduced in 1903, in time for them to imprint themselves on the imagination of James Joyce before he went into exile. In *Ulysses*, he writes: 'A bag of fig rolls lay snugly in Armstrong's satchel. He curled them between his palms at whiles and swallowed them safely. Crumbs adhered to the tissues of his lips. A sweetened boy's breath.'

Joyce must have liked fig rolls. Personally, I think they are a bit of an austerity biscuit – a reminder of a simpler and much less fun era.

Notice that young Armstrong had a bag of fig rolls, not a packet. Biscuits used to be sold loose in those days. I can just about remember this in practice at the Monument Creamery in Drumcondra. Jacob's had a fine glazed biscuit cabinet, from the depths of which fig rolls and other delights would be seized and transferred to the weighing scales. 'A pound of biscuits' is the kind of thing my grandmother would have had on her shopping list.

Incidentally, it was never revealed if Jim Figgerty put the figs into fig rolls or merely was privy to the great secret of how it was done. This has allowed a later generation of advertising folk to spoil the whole thing by having an animated child reveal that it's all down to aliens. This claim has been greeted with considerable scepticism, even amongst six-year-olds.

Jam

I sometimes wonder how many people go to the trouble of making jam at home. These days, when you can buy all sorts of good-quality stuff off the shelf, it seems like a lot of trouble, but the jam-making tradition stretches back to when this was an obvious and useful way of preserving the crop. Jam was, and to some extent still is, thrifty. Maybe home jam-making took a big hit during the days of the Celtic Tiger, when it was fashionable to whip up a dish of grilled prawns with sweet chilli sauce but not so zeitgeisty to slave over a cauldron of boiling raspberries.

My mother was a jam and marmalade maker. The raspberry crop – what we didn't manage to eat of it with a bit of sugar and lashings of cream – was preserved in this way for the dark, cold winter days: a taste of summer. And every January, during that little window of opportunity when the Seville oranges were available, the kitchen (indeed, the whole house) would be pungent with the scent of citrus and hot sugar.

We were not slavish enthusiasts for jam, no matter how good it was. Indeed, a lot of our raspberry jam went into queen of puddings. In our house, this comprised a kind of egg-custard base flavoured with orange rind (not the more usual lemon, possibly for reasons of thrift), topped with jam and then topped again with soft meringue peaks. It was, and still is, one of the best sweet things you can eat.

So great was our demand for raspberry jam as a result of this that the home-made supply would occasionally run out. And then a jar of Fruitfield, from Lamb Brothers, would appear. Occasionally it might be one of Tiptree's 'preserves'.

Marmalade, on the other hand, was consumed in almost industrial quantities at breakfast-time. Spread thickly on batch toast.

My mother, like most housewives of the time, didn't have a freezer. I don't think it was merely a question of cost (early deep-freezes cost a king's ransom in those days): I have a feeling she may not have entirely trusted them. We were something of a Luddite household, mistrustful of technology.

It may seem strange, but I always associate jam-making with the winter months now that freezers are all over the place. We tend to freeze our fruit as it is picked and then make jam in fairly small batches as we need it.

There's something very pleasant about having the kitchen filled with the scent of strawberries or raspberries in the depths of November, a lovely sense of summer (or what passes for it in Ireland) as the winter rain lashes against the window-panes.

There are several reasons behind our winter jam work. The summer is busy enough as it is without doing all that boiling and jar-sterilising. But also, there's the question of how some fruits, and some jams, behave. Strawberry jam has a tendency to lose colour, so it makes sense to use it within a couple of months of when it is made.

The strawberry, of course, makes one of the most desirable jams, simply the best with croissants, and almost unrivalled in a queen of puddings. But among jam-makers the strawberry is dreaded for one major reason: a tendency to be somewhat deficient in pectin, the substance that aids setting. For many people, strawberry jam ends up being unacceptably runny, and some people's versions are so liquid that the stuff has to be drunk rather than eaten.

Now, you can either accept that this is the way that strawberry jam is meant to be, or you can take certain cunning steps to boost the pectin levels. Commercial jam-makers work in something like laboratory conditions, measuring levels of enzymes and natural sugars and what have you, and adjusting accordingly. In the domestic kitchen, we just have to take it as read that every batch of jam will be different. Boosting the pectin level when you are using strawberries or apricots, for example, can have unexpected results. It is possible, for example, to end up with a jam that is so unrunny, to coin a phrase, that it has the consistency of a fruit gum. Now, I realise that some people like a stiff jam, but there are limits.

If you want a well-behaved jam – one that is liquid enough for pleasure but which manages to stay on the spoon while you transfer it from the jar to the toast, stick with raspberries. They are more tart than strawberries, and tartness always seems to go with good setting.

Harold McGee, in his encyclopaedic *On Food and Cooking*, says that jam works because 'like salt, sugar makes the fruit inhospitable to microbes'. Jam, he says, is all about 'the nature of pectin, one of the components of the plant cell wall, and its fortuitous interaction with the fruit's acids and the cook's added sugar'.

If you need to boost pectin levels in strawberry jam (and if you like it stiff, this is essential), peel the yellow skin thinly off a lemon, leaving as much of the white pith as possible. Then slice up the lemon and put it in with the fruit as it cooks.

Whenever I cook jam, it's a comforting experience. For a start, it feels like a sensible and worthwhile thing to do, even if the amount of sugar involved can look quite frightening. But there's also a pleasant sense of tradition: that you are there, in your rightful place, in a long line of jam-makers. It's a good feeling.

Christmas pudding

My paternal grandmother was, by all accounts, a formidable lady. She died when I was four, and my memories of her are very hazy. I have a vague idea that she was tall and thin and constantly swathed in black garments. Quite scary, really.

Despite her own modest upbringing, she was distantly related, on her father's side, to the great Admiral Beatty, who, as the historically minded will recall, adopted a firm line at the Battle of Jutland during World War One. Beatty, who was made an earl for his trouble, was born in County Wexford and went to school in Kilkenny before rising to the very top of what was then the world's greatest naval service.

Well, as they say, it's not off the stones he licked it. The Beattys, if these two very remote cousins were anything to go by, were not to be trifled with.

The only recorded occasion on which my grandmother's composure deserted her was when she ran an errand for my mother, who was in the middle of the very involved process – indeed, ritual – of making the Christmas puddings at the time. Mind you, she only had herself to blame because, in a moment of uncharacteristic charm, she volunteered to pick up one of the key ingredients.

And so it was that my grandmother, one November day in the late 1950s, ended up entering the public bar of the Cat & Cage in Drumcondra, in search of a bottle of Guinness. It was just after opening time, and I suspect that the curate (as barmen were called in those days) gave her a broad wink as she placed her order. But before my grand-mother could shout 'Stop', he had opened the bottle and poured the black stuff into a glass. She nearly passed away, being the kind of person who (a) did not frequent licensed premises, and (b) confined her drinking to a small glass of A Winter's Tale before Christmas dinner.

Guinness, you see, was an essential ingredient in the family Christmas pudding. As was Powers whiskey, which was the default spirit in our teetotal household, despite the fact that my mother always maintained that it made my nor-mally mild-mannered grandfather cranky and keen to ques-tion the parenthood of the founders of the state. Powers brought out the Southern unionist in him.

Anyway, there was much more to the Christmas pud-ding. There was a great deal of butter, at least the same quantity of suet, a mountain of dried fruit, oceans of breadcrumbs, handfuls of grated carrot, and enough spices to stock an old-fashioned apothecary's shop.

It was great stuff but, like the smell of Bewley's coffee roasting (as it did in those days – it was the key smell of Grafton Street), the ritual of preparation was even better than the consumption. I suppose the mixing took only a day but in memory it seems to have dragged on for the bet-ter part of a week. There was probably soaking and mari-nating involved. I can't recall.

And then, literally for days (and nights), the emulsion-painted kitchen walls dripped constantly with condensation as the boiling was done. This involved a great deal of steam – so much, that it was hard to see where the cooker was. And a kettle that was always ready to top up the water in the bubbling pots. It was a Trojan effort.

The consumption of the resulting pudding (of which many were made and either stored or given away) was always a bit of a trial on Christmas Day. This was the kind of pudding that could, literally, claim to be a meal in itself.

Christmas dinner would invariably start with prawn cocktail, complete with Marie Rose sauce, finely chopped lettuce and the compulsory sprinkling of paprika on top. Then the turkey and two kinds of stuffing, sprouts, roast potatoes, bread sauce and gravy. And then, penultimately, the pudding.

It was a solid pudding, the kind that came not so much in slices as in ingots. The substance, the weight, the solidity owes much, no doubt, to the amount of fruit it contained, and the pounds upon pounds of butter that went into it.

The pudding was served – a little half-heartedly, it has to be said – with whipped cream, never brandy butter, in our virtually alcohol-free household. And then came the Christmas cake, which was enrobed in a good inch of home-made marzipan – or 'almond paste', as we always called it. And a further outer coating of sugar icing, which my mother always sharpened up with some lemon juice.

It was in the days after Christmas, however, that the pudding came into its own. Thick slices would be fried gently in butter until the outside became lightly caramelised, then they would be doused in cold cream or lathered with Bird's Custard.

The Christmas-morning repast was taken after Midnight Mass, at about 1 AM. For some long-lost reason, this meal always kicked off with grapefruit, an item so exotic in those days that it usually came in a large tin. At no other time of the year did we brave the acidic tang of this austere citrus fruit, but at Christmas it was compulsory. Needless to say, it was followed by bacon, sausages, eggs and both black and white pudding.

My mother was generous with love, and food was just one expression of it. Particularly at Christmas.